The Paradox of Mental Health

The Paradox of Mental Health

Toward Systemic and Social Constructionist Therapies

Raphael J. Becvar, Dorothy Stroh Becvar,
and Lynne V. Reif

Forewords by
Benjamin J. Evans, Johnny Faulkner,
and Amy Smith

ROWMAN & LITTLEFIELD
Lanham • Boulder • New York • London

Published by Rowman & Littlefield
An imprint of The Rowman & Littlefield Publishing Group, Inc.
4501 Forbes Boulevard, Suite 200, Lanham, Maryland 20706
www.rowman.com

86-90 Paul Street, London EC2A 4NE

British Library Cataloguing in Publication Information Available

Library of Congress Cataloging-in-Publication Data

Includes bibliographic references and index.
ISBN: 979-8-8818-0223-3 (cloth)
ISBN: 979-8-8818-0224-0 (paperback)
ISBN: 979-8-8818-0225-7 (electronic)

To John Steven Reif Jr.,
Jonathan Garland,
Carlysle Garland, and Darien Garland,
and to Dorothy S. Becvar,
for whom there was and is only connectedness.
May her wisdom and faith continue to inspire.

Contents

Forewords ix

Acknowledgments xiii

Introduction xv

**PART I: PARADOXES OF MENTAL HEALTH AND
ILLNESS: PHILOSOPHY AND THEORY** **1**

1 The Paradox of Mental Health: On the Limits of Living
Consciously 3

2 Believing Is Seeing: Exploring the Limits of Knowing 13

3 Before the Beginning 23

4 Contributions from Social Science and Mental Health
Professionals 37

5 On the Clinical Bias 43

6 Conceptual Bites in Summary of the Paradox 47

7 Wondering 53

**PART II: SYSTEMIC AND SOCIAL CONSTRUCTIONIST
CONCEPTS AND PROCESSES FOR THERAPY** **61**

8 About Systems Theory, Constructivism, and Social
Constructionism 63

9 Requiem for Systemic Marital and Family Therapy 73

10 The Ecosystemic Story: Implications for Therapists 85

11 Reflections on Values in Systems Theory and Social
Constructionism 95

12 A Story about Systemic and Social Constructionist Therapy 103

Afterword 109

References 113

Index 117

About the Authors 125

Forewords

In my high school senior English class, we covered Greek mythology as it was collected in Edith Hamilton's book *Mythology*. Greek mythology is a fascinating collection of explanatory myths that pepper and pervade our culture. It is part of the Weltanschauung in which we are born. As a result, we have Herculean tasks, we are struck by Cupid's arrow, we have Hermeneutic analyses, we experience monotony alongside Sisyphus, we worry about flying too close to the sun like Icarus, and we are aware of the dangers inherent in the opening Pandora's box. I've remained intrigued by these myths for almost thirty years now. One of the most fascinating characters to me then and now is Procrustes.

In Greek mythology, Procrustes would invite travelers weary from the road to spend the night in his guest room. Once inside his home, Procrustes would either stretch them to fit the bed, or if they were too tall, he would amputate to make them fit, not considering the effects of his winnowing. The metaphor of the Procrustean bed has been used for ages now to describe a winnowing machine of conformity that pays little attention to what it is winnowing. The medical model of mental health is such a Procrustean bed. It is a grisly black box, where an outside expert does something to a passive patient.

What Ray and Lynne, along with the spirit of Dorothy, have done across these vibrant pages is to remind us that we are not separate from what we observe and that it is us who winnow whom we watch into what is normal or abnormal. This is, of course, not a new idea, but it is as relevant today as it was when the authors stated simply and clearly, "Let us first do no harm" (Becvar et al., 1982, p. 391). This is not a passive thing done out there; it is an active thing we do every time we meet with someone in our work. It is a choice that requires "conscious effort to be cybernetic in thought and action" (Ray, 2005, p. 361).

Systems theory, punctuated here as social constructionism and second-order cybernetics, is part of the epistemology that has an awareness of itself. I would be remiss if I didn't mention that the word *cybernetics* comes from the Greek word *kubernetes*, meaning "steersman, one who turns or steers a vessel" (Beer, 2004, p. 857). Bringing or rebringing a social constructionist and/or second-order cybernetic perspective to mental health is the steering or turning of the therapeutic view that is needed in our increasingly winnowed world of mental health and mental illness. This is the Gordian knot that is the paradox of mental health that Ray and Lynne, along with the spiritual presence of Dorothy, are trying to cut.

I can't help but to be reminded of Don Jackson's paper "The Myth of Normality" and the "insidious influence" that normality exerts on our society (Jackson, 2009, p. 218). It was the very first paper I was assigned in my master's program. Originally published in 1967, it still resonates as the expansion of diagnostic criteria has exploded since the first *DSM* was published in the 1950s. Also assigned was Ray and Dorothy's book *Family Therapy: A Systemic Integration*. It seems as though their voices have always been with me as I've transitioned from graduate student to professional. At this point in my career, I am an assistant professor in charge of the Don Jackson Archive at the University of Louisiana, Monroe, and I am writing a foreword to the new book by Ray, Lynne, and the spirit of Dorothy. The circularity that I am punctuating is palpable. I cannot wait to share these vital pages with current, future, and former students, and I can only begin to imagine how often I myself will turn and return to them as I take Ray, Lynne, and Dorothy's suggestion to reflect on and think about how I think.

Benjamin J. Evans
AAMFT Approved Supervisor
Assistant Professor, University of Louisiana, Monroe

Ray and Dorothy and Lynne Reif's love and commitment to fellow humans and to the ecosystem paradigm has long been known by those fortunate to be in their company. Prolific authors, teachers, and mentors on this subject and other related areas, their book *The Paradox of Mental Health* is, in my estimation, of crucial importance at this time.

Problems as typically understood are in peril in this work. Throughout this book, Ray, Dorothy, and Lynne suggest that problems are implicitly embedded in everyday life and are found in the stories we have of ourselves and of others. These stories evolve from professional psychological discourse.

The authors challenge some basic concepts and practices of professional therapy based on the normative, medical model. They suggest that therapy based on the medical model may contribute to the increasing numbers of people who are diagnosed as or experience themselves as mentally ill. They suggest that therapy models need to change so that the helping professions can be effective without creating more problems. The authors thoughtfully provoke the reader to take a journey that explores the limits of the conceptual frameworks in the education of professional therapists. Readers should be prepared for a roller-coaster ride of challenging and enlightening evidence of the cocreation of problems as self-serving solutions that may increase the problems that people experience.

As a therapy on therapy, the ideas they share are metaconcepts outside the typical scope and practice of the helping professions. By suggesting we look beyond the horizon of the medical-model approach, they present systems theory and social constructionism as the paradigms for a rethinking of the therapy profession. The implications are breathtaking, as systems theory and social constructionism offer unique concepts and practices applicable to all levels of system—from individual to international relationships. Weaving concepts of quantum physics, cybernetics, and systems theory, they present a relatable and pragmatic approach to apply in individual, family, and societal therapies.

Their plea within the text is one of import: that the reader consider the limitations of the normative, medical-model paradigm and the unintentional pain created when attempts to solve problems and conflicts may contribute to more serious problems. They suggest that problems when viewed in context are logical, normal adaptations within the contexts of which they are a part. Human beings are a part of the entire ecosystem; they are one with the ecosystem, as are therapists who would help clients become "normal." Therein is a paradox—the attempt to help people become "normal" in contexts in which their experience of mental illness is a normal response or adaptation. The authors' ideas plant seeds and offer practical suggestions for therapeutic practice that can mitigate unnecessary pain and suggest a meta-awareness view of problems in context as opportunities for growth.

Representing collectively more than a century of wisdom, teaching experience, and long-term perspective, Ray, Dorothy, and Lynne offer the reader an easily digestible set of ideas that has the potential to safely and lovingly bring much-needed new energy to those who commit themselves every day to helping others and teaching others to help more effectively. As they wrote in 1982, "Let Us First Do No Harm."

Johnny Faulkner
Director, the Haelan Centers
Archivist, the collected works of Virginia Satir

I first encountered Dr. Ray Becvar while completing my internship as a therapist. Over the course of two years, I and fellow students and colleagues actively participated in biweekly meetings led by Dr. Becvar. Through the process of case consultation and Q and A, Dr. Becvar taught basic systems-theory concepts as applied to therapy. These conversations prompted a discernible shift in my perspective. I increasingly recognized the difference between the medical model that was taught in my master's program and the systemic framework advocated by Dr. Becvar. Guided by his mentorship and our subsequent email exchanges, while not discounting the potential utility of my formal education, I have embraced the principles of the systems model in almost all of my clinical work and my life.

Upon learning that Dr. Becvar and Lynne Reif had authored *The Paradox of Mental Health*, I eagerly anticipated the opportunity to delve into the concepts that had been the focus of our biweekly consultations. With Lynne's inclusion in our meetings during this period, I welcomed the chance to familiarize myself with her insights and perspectives. Additionally, I was pleased to hear the voice of Dr. Dorothy Becvar, Dr. Ray Becvar's esteemed late wife, who continues to be heard in the book.

After completing this book, it became evident to me that in the vast landscape of mental health literature, there are works that merely scratch the surface, and then there are those rare gems that compel us to dive deeper, questioning the very foundations on which our understanding rests. This book, penned by the insightful Drs. Ray and Dorothy Becvar and Lynne Reif, belongs firmly in the latter category. As I delved into these pages, I found myself not just reading but also embarking on a journey of introspection and inquiry. The Becvars and Reif possess a remarkable ability to challenge conventional wisdom with a blend of profound insight and genuine empathy.

In this explication of systems theory and the paradox of mental health, the Becvars and Reif fearlessly confront the limitations of our normative, medical model, which dominates clinical practice. Through thoughtful analysis and thought-provoking questions, they compel us to reconsider the complex interplay between individual psychology, societal structures, and cultural norms.

But what truly sets this work apart is its call to action. The Becvars and Reif do not merely point out flaws; they challenge mental health practitioners to examine their own roles in constructing and perpetuating the problems they treat. It is a call for introspection, accountability, and ultimately progress in reducing the incidence of people experiencing and being diagnosed with mental illness.

Prepare to be challenged and inspired and above all to embark on a journey of self-discovery, for in these pages, you will not find direct solutions but rather the seeds of transformation.

Amy Smith
Mental Health Counselor, the Haelan Centers

Acknowledgments

We give thanks to those individuals, couples, students, and families with whom we have worked and whom we have endeavored to help experience happier lives. We also give thanks once again to our students, trainees, and colleagues, whose provocative questions pushed us to think more clearly and to present our ideas in a clear and understandable manner. Finally, we wish to thank those professors, students, and practitioners who have found our books and articles to be a meaningful addition to their professional and personal lives. We hope this book serves that purpose, as well. Special thanks also to the team at Bloomsbury for their fine work and assistance with bringing this book to fruition, including Sarah Rinehart, Christopher Fischer, Niki Guinan, and Jonathan Joyce.

Introduction

Therapy can be constructively viewed as an opportunity to learn or to grow. Crisis and opportunity are complements.

—Dorothy Stroh Becvar

In these chapters, we explore a pair of analogies:

A. As human behavior at times becomes self-defeating and in need of psychotherapy, so sometimes do human concepts stand in need of therapy.
B. In somewhat the sense in which theories of psychotherapy express forms of therapy that are used to treat self-defeating behaviors, so is a general epistemological therapy for dysfunctional concepts possible. (Bartlett, 1983, p. 21)

We key on Bartlett's assertion that a "general epistemological therapy for dysfunctional concepts is possible." We amend this as follows: A general therapy for dysfunctional concepts and processes of social science and mental health therapy is possible. It is our belief that many concepts and practices in the social sciences and mental health field "stand in need of therapy." The therapy models we choose to diagnose to be in need of therapy are the concepts of normative, medical-model(s) theories and practices of therapy. The therapy models we select to treat the normative, medical models are systems theory and social constructionism. Systems theory and social construction are suggested as the antidote to what we believe to be a pandemic of mental illness.

These chapters do therapy on the normative, medical model of therapy that dominates therapeutic practice. Practitioners using the normative, medical model may not believe their model is in need of therapy. The normative, medical model is internally consistent and purports to offer solutions to what we believe is a pandemic of mental illness. We share the symptoms of conceptual illness that we observe. Here is our story.

The COVID-19 pandemic, also known as the coronavirus pandemic, is an ongoing pandemic of coronavirus disease 2019 (COVID-19) caused by severe acute respiratory syndrome coronavirus 2 (SARS-CoV-2). It was first identified in December 2019 in Wuhan. The coronavirus is a virus. It is a protein and amino acid. It is a parasite. It feeds on its hosts and in the process destroys them. Millions of people were affected in the world, and millions died after being infected.

We suggest that we are in the throes of another pandemic—a pandemic of mental illness. Indeed, according to the National Institute of Mental Health (2023), "it is estimated that more than one in five U.S. adults live with a mental illness (57.8 million in 2021)." There is no physical virus in the mental health pandemic, but we believe there are what we call conceptual viruses—no less virulent than the COVID-19 virus. These conceptual viruses spread from person to person via professional and social discourse. The concepts in professional medical-model discourse bleed into social discourse, which includes conversations about mental health and mental illness. Using concepts and constructs from professional discourse, people monitor themselves and others for "symptoms" and deviations from "normal" behavior or experiences based on values of society. These deviations or symptoms are often interpreted as evidence of mental illness or "disorders" in need of "treatment"—usually talk therapy or medication. Other efforts to stem the pandemic of mental illness are focused on prevention. Designating a month for mental health awareness is an attempt to bring awareness to and prevent mental illness, thereby attempting to slow down the pandemic. Checklists of what one should do and not do, articles about how to prevent mental illness or promote mental health, suggestions for increased monitoring of self or others, and support groups are attempts at prevention. All of these well-intentioned efforts to thwart the reality of the pandemic are logically consistent with the hnormative, medical model. This model is supported ideologically, politically, and economically.

The medical model served us well enough during the COVID-19 pandemic, but we suggest that the medical model used in professional mental health discourse and treatment may not be serving us well with the pandemic of mental illness. Indeed, it may not only be not serving us well, but also the solutions it offers to stem the mental health pandemic may be contributing to the increased incidence of mental illness. Foulkes and Andrews (2023) posit a call to action to investigate what they term as a "prevalence inflation hypothesis," which suggests that "increased awareness and overinterpretation" of disease and dysfunction are contributing to a rise in identification of mental illness (p. 2). A recent article in the *New York Times* about the rise in depression in adolescents notes that current research is bearing out the news that in many cases, attempts at intervention and treatment for mental health issues in teens are in fact backfiring, exacerbating the presenting issues rather than calming them (Saxby, 2023). From the systems perspective, the methods of "treatment" based on the medical model may be described as what Wátzlawick et al. (1974) refer to as attempted first-order change—change attempted at the wrong level or change attempted without or with a limited view of the context in which problems evolve.

The problem is, despite all efforts at slowing or stopping the pandemic of mental illness, the numbers of people defined as and experiencing mental illness continue to increase. We suggest that these well-intentioned efforts from within the logic of this normative, medical model paradoxically may be contributing to the escalation of numbers of people experiencing themselves and others as mentally ill.

From the systems perspective, there are pathologies of epistemology in the paradigm of the normative, medical model that contribute to its participation in making the "problem" worse. These include the beliefs that

- You can do just one thing without affecting other things in a totally conjoined universe.
- The map is the territory; the model describes the way things really are; concepts and constructs become reified.
- Control is possible—particularly unilateral control in relationships that, by definition, are bilateral.
- You can just observe without affecting that which you observe—a Newtonian physics view rather than a quantum physics view that the observer affects what she observes in unpredictable ways.
- People are autonomous, independent entities. Thus, the individual is the primary unit of analysis. They are viewed independent of contexts that necessarily include them.
- Problems and reality exist out there instead of problems reflecting values of societies and being implicit in the worldviews of societies.

As mentioned earlier, these are pathologies of epistemology only from the systems perspective. But these pathologies have dire consequences when ignored in any model. We suggest that if normative, medical-model practitioners respected these pathologies and altered their practices accordingly, then the slowing or eliminating of the pandemic of mental illness would be possible. This book elaborates on this and suggests that therapeutic practice based on systems theory and social constructionism would be more effective.

This would require that therapeutic practitioners have an "epistemology that has a conscious awareness of itself" and help their clients develop one, as well. Indeed, people living with conscious awareness of pathologies of epistemology in their worldviews may help them experience and live life very differently. They would believe that

- Everything they do or do not do cannot not affect other people, creatures, and things.
- The worldview in which they live and live for is but one of many possible worldviews or stories.
- Their attempts to control will paradoxically give them less control than if they let things run their course. Also, attempts to unilaterally control that which is bilateral or multilateral will fail and have unforeseen and often dire consequences. The concept and belief that we can control is an illusion.
- As they observe, they cannot not affect that which they are observing. They would be aware that the person they are observing is affected by their observation and is observing them observing them. Their relationship is a miniature social system—the two are one.
- All people, creatures, and things in this totally conjoined universe are connected, and together they comprise context—one system. To observe a person independent of context is a very limited view. Observing a person in different contexts provides different views and stories. They would be aware that how people are with them is relative to how they are with them and vice versa.

The business of therapy is thriving. Indeed, when large corporations get involved, their marketing efforts have an investment in increasing the numbers of people seeking therapy. When artificial intelligence gets into the therapy market, it requires standardized diagnoses, standardized problems, and standardized therapeutic treatments to help people adapt to follow standardized rules and ways to live in society. The normative, medical model has these available and prepackaged. There does not seem to be much room for individuality. We may be losing our right not to conform.

Listen to the following conversation between Gregory Bateson (1972) and his daughter Mary Catherine:

DAUGHTER: I did an experiment once.

FATHER: Yes?

DAUGHTER: I wanted to find out if I could think two thoughts at the same time, so I thought, "It's summer," and I thought, "It's winter." And then I tried to think the two thoughts together.

Father: Yes?

Daughter: But I found I wasn't having two thoughts. I was having one thought about two thoughts. (p. 2)

Indeed, one cannot think about mental health without thinking about mental illness. Thus, attempts to prevent mental illness and/or promote mental health cannot not activate self-conscious wondering about one's mental health and illness. What are the limits of monitoring ourselves and living self-consciously? Don't think about the elephant on the table.

We wonder what problems people would experience—whether people would experience problems—or how would they story their experience if the language and concepts or constructs of professional mental illness categories did not exist. These categories find their way into social discourse. Indeed, many of the metaphors used to name disorders have only recently been constructed. In the 1950s, the number of disorders in the *DSM* was 60. Now there are hundreds, with new candidates constructed and voted to be included with each new version of the *DSM*. With what stories (metaphors) did people call their experiences without the most recent constructions?

We wonder about utility of the concept of mental illness per se. The word *mental* locates the problem within the individual and excludes the context from which problems evolve—not caused. We wonder about this when it is applied to what can be conceived as common life transitions and challenges. Life happens. How a phenomenon is named brings forth that reality. We don't relate to people. We relate to the stories we tell ourselves about people—and each metaphor or construct activates a story. Current social discourse is replete with stories of deviation and deficiency reflecting professional normative, medical-model discourse. Yes, life happens, but the happenings of life are also love, joy, happiness, and fulfillment.

We now suggest what might not be viewed as serious, but it fits our message. The idea is not new; Thomas Szasz (1970) suggested something similar. Because more and more people are experiencing and diagnosing themselves and others as being mentally ill, we can cure them all at once by diagnosing all people as mentally ill. This should not be hard because everybody can point to at least one experience each day that makes one wonder about their sanity as well as that of others. Thus, "mental illness" becomes normal—the concept self-destructs—except for the diagnosticians. We diagnosticians could diagnose ourselves as mentally ill, but in so doing, we lose our credibility as "expert" diagnosticians who use "objective scientific" criteria to make our diagnosis. In essence, as subjective beings, we cannot objectively diagnose ourselves—or anybody else. We wonder who would be the therapists to treat the diagnosticians—their normalcy would be abnormal.

Don Jackson (2009) wrote,

> I submit that there is no such thing as a normal person. Instead, there is a wide variety of adaptive patterns and behavioral repertoires. How a person acts varies with the culture, the subculture, the ethnic group, and the family group in which he lives. We tend to forget that values change, because we are uplifting the new and forgetting the old. (p. 222)

Of course, if there is no such thing as a normal person, then there is no such thing as an abnormal person. Let us move on. We have shown our hand about what these chapters are about—directly and indirectly.

This book is divided into two parts. Part I focuses on what we call the paradox of mental illness. These chapters suggest that therapy theory and practice consistent with the medical model is contributing to the increasing incidence of mental illness. One chapter presents our view of the systems perspective and social constructionism. Part II focuses on explicating systems theory and social constructionism and provides concepts for therapy and the education of therapists from these perspectives.

All therapy involves relationships—yes, even psychopharmaceutical treatments. At base, systems theory is about relationships—between people, between concepts, and between institutions. Social constructionism is about stories. Indeed, the very process of knowing (i.e., drawing distinctions) necessarily involves relationships. Relationships are everything—especially life. Systems theory is a social construction. Yes, social construction is a social construction. It is about knowledge of knowledge.

FOR THE READER

Please know that these chapters were written at different times in our careers for different purposes. Indeed, this is not a new concern for us. In 1982, Ray and Dorothy wrote a lead article in the _Journal of Marital and Family Therapy_, "Let Us First Do No Harm." You will notice that the majority of our citations are from earlier times. Unfortunately, literature written about epistemology and from the systemic perspective has been lacking in recent years. We hope this book helps to bring systems thinking back to the forefront, for the perspective it offers is powerful.

Keep in mind that each chapter offers another element or layer of our general theme; while each could stand alone as its own document, there is a continuity in the order in which we arrange them. There are many conversations within the field of therapy, but there are not enough conversations _about_ the field of therapy. By sharing these chapters with you, it is our hope that readers might develop an "epistemology that has a conscious awareness of itself," or knowledge about knowledge and how we know. This book offers a model for both training and practice. Let us first do no harm in our efforts to be helpful. Indeed, any model that is potentially therapeutic is also potentially toxic—including the model we propose.

Please note that we use the word *therapist* throughout this book as a general designation for all practicing clinicians, including counselors, social workers, psychologists, marriage and family therapists, clergy, and so on. You will also notice repetition in some of the chapters. Please bear with these redundancies. We wrote of similar concepts in different clothes for different purposes at different times. Perhaps as you read, the following sentiment will resonate: "[R]epetition is what allows something brand new to occur. Repetition, like the lapping of ripples against a rock, gently shifts the ground on which we tread, and so alters our relationship to the things we experience" (Klein, 2016, p. 71).

Part I

PARADOXES OF MENTAL HEALTH AND ILLNESS

PHILOSOPHY AND THEORY

Chapter 1

The Paradox of Mental Health

On the Limits of Living Consciously

As a function of several societal forces, some basically altruistic and some more market driven, consumers of radio, TV, social media, books, and journals are the recipients of a barrage of information about health and mental health and their warning signals. Most recently, there is a growing concern about the effects of the pandemic on the mental health of people whose usual lifestyles were significantly interrupted and required radical change. Of course, whenever there is a barrage of information about mental illness (and physical illness), people tend to be more self-conscious about their own mental health and illness as well as conscious about the mental health of others. Self-consciousness has always been an important mandate in any society's social control mechanisms. Every society would have its members self-consciously monitor themselves and monitor others' conformity to the ways of "right" living required for membership in any culture or society.

Indeed, self-consciousness and other consciousness is very important in any society. These are part of the process of socialization or, might we say, domestication in any society or culture. It starts very early in life. Næss (with Haukeland, 2002) described the beginning as follows: The formation of a mask is beginning. "What I really think and feel I will keep to myself." But "[w]hen it finally dawns on the child that she is being watched, her natural reaction appears to be shyness" (p. 43). Her behavior may evolve into a performance for the watching audience.

Ah, the mask. The mask, of course, is not demonstrating overtly that one is self-consciously monitoring oneself or monitoring others. To make meaning of what we are writing, it is important to realize that the concept "self-conscious" as we conceive it means being conscious of the self that one is presenting to the public as well as the higher-order self that is monitoring the self that one is presenting for public consumption. Indeed, almost any social

3

context requires a degree of self-consciousness, as one would complement the dynamics of the many social contexts to which one belongs in this life. It has to do with relationship(s). We find it useful to think that every dyadic relationship is a miniature society and requires a certain degree of self-monitoring and reading the context about how to be in that context. Of course, there may be a relationship in which one feels a "natural fit" or feels no need to self-consciously monitor oneself in that relationship. One can feel free to just "let it all hang out." Perhaps it is a relationship in which neither person seeks to prevail. Of course, this assessment implies a self-consciousness that one need not be self-conscious in this relationship.

"It seems as if some people never have the feeling of being observed" (Næss with Haukeland, 2002, p. 43). They are so engrossed in a project that they do not experience being observed. Also, a person who has been well-socialized into a culture may perform the social rituals of the society without doing so self-consciously. Almost all social rituals within a society are learned by participation and observation, not formal instruction. Indeed, almost everything we learn for living is learned via participation, observation, and internalizing "context markers"—those subtle, almost imperceptible social cues about how to be in a social context. In effect, we may become conscious of the ritualistic social protocols only when we violate one. Then self-consciousness begins—and perhaps embarrassment. We wonder if we can ever shut this process down. Can we ever not be self-conscious of our self-consciousness. Sometimes we try, but we do so at our own peril (i.e., we risk becoming a topic of conversation). Indeed, in authoritarian societies, constant self-consciousness and monitoring of others never stops. There is no spontaneity. Others are watching. Thus, we must watch ourselves. Indeed, there may be an authoritarian aspect to any relationship—as others watch and diagnose and those watched watch and diagnose the watchers.

So where are we going with this? Good question. *We believe that while self-consciousness is necessary, overly scrupulous self-consciousness of one's state of mental illness and health can paradoxically lead one to believe that one is mentally ill.* Of course, one must have the concept of mental illness and health and its complementary *DSM* categories in one's conceptual repertoire to come up with such a self-assessment. And we are socialized to believe that there are objective standards by which one can make such a diagnosis—a belief that we believe has validity or merit only within that conceptual model. Mental illness and health experts, as well as those who have been diagnosed by these experts, will challenge this statement, of course. Thus, people engage in rigorous, critical self-scrutiny of themselves and their relationships. Alan Watts (1972) presents an analogy that describes the process of overly critical self-scrutiny and attempts to live a too finely honed life that successfully prevents happiness. In a live television performance, Watts instructed the cameraman to turn the camera on the monitor, thereby creating an oscillation pattern on the monitor. Watts advised the viewing audience that there is nothing wrong with their TV sets and said, "We are looking at what we are doing so closely we get all these jitters. And that's what happens when you get anxious. You will also get these jitters when you look at what you are doing too closely" (Watts & Moore, 1959).

Aha! That is the paradox of which we write. If you believe in the concept of mental illness, you certainly will see it and perhaps experience it or wonder if you "qualify." If you don't, then probably not. We suggest that "mental illness" is a social construct treated as something "real." We wonder, where in the body is the "mental" located. But it is real to those who believe in it and who tell themselves a mental illness story about their experience and the experience of others. Let's revisit the first sentence of this chapter: As a function of several societal forces, some basically altruistic and some more market driven, consumers of radio, TV, social media, books, and journals are the recipients of a barrage of information about health and mental health and their warning signals.

Continuing. On the one hand, there are those who believe that prevention of problems is best achieved through education about signs and symptoms, checklists for personal assessment, dire warnings about what ignoring such potential problems could mean, and participation in activities designed to preclude their occurrence. On the other hand (only two hands), there are those whose main goal is to sell a book, model, program, or certification in the true spirit of entrepreneurship. But regardless of motivation, the outcome is the same: a heightened awareness about problems and increased sensitivity to anything that could be construed as an indicator of that problem.

However, these efforts at prevention do not seem to have been success-ful in reducing the incidence of problems in the mental health field. Thus, our goal in this chapter is to consider, by asking different questions, how we might do a better job of finding solutions to some persistently insoluble and even escalating frequency of problems, both in our society and in other societies of the world. *That is, consistent with Watts (1972), we suggest that problems that are persistently insoluble (or escalating) should be suspected as questions asked in the wrong way.*

We undertake this process of positing different assumptions and questions:

A. As human behavior at times becomes self-defeating and in need of psy-chotherapy, so sometimes do human concepts stand in need of therapy.
B. In somewhat the sense in which theories of psychotherapy express forms of therapy that are used to treat self-defeating behaviors, so is a general epistemological therapy for dysfunctional concepts possible. (Bartlett, 1983, p. 21).

As part of an attempt at conceptual therapy relative to the mental health field, we ask whether our efforts at normal mental health practice and normal science paradoxically are eroding the sense of well-being that we strive for and seek to enhance. We begin by suggesting that perhaps physical symptoms and emotional or relationship malaise do not necessarily describe problems in need of solution. We also suggest that the malaise itself may be a product of a finely honed sensitivity to one's experience of self and one's relationships, a sensitivity that we professionals have encouraged, attempting to be helpful. That is, as we give people explanations or raised "red flags" about symptoms or emotional or relationship issues, our explanations can serve to create problems or more serious problems. Moreover, this heightened sensitivity may be akin to a contagious disease, as malaise can spread rapidly though a population via social, medical, and educational discourses, which become conversations we have about ourselves and conversations we have with others about ourselves and those they have with us. A pandemic?

Virginia Satir (1967) has noted that it is not our feelings that are the problem but our feelings about our feelings that can become problematic, for the kind of feelings we have about our feelings is relative to the explanation we have about our feelings. Thus, if we tell ourselves and/or others tell us that we should not feel depressed and consciously try to get rid of our depression, then not only are we depressed, but also now we feel guilty for not being able to not be depressed. We cannot consciously control that which occurs spontaneously. Thus, we become depressed about our depression. The problem is not depression but our depression about our depression.

Into each life some depression, anxiety, and worry will come—life happens. Thomas Szasz (1970) wrote, "The concept of mental illness thus serves mainly to obscure the everyday fact that life for most people is a continuous struggle, nor for biological survival, but for a 'place in the sun, 'peace of mind' or some other meaning or value" (pp. 22–23).

We cannot control these natural responses to life's circumstances. Feelings are not subject to mind-over-matter conscious control. Attempts to do so will fail. Thus, we put people in a "be-spontaneous" paradox (Wátzlawick et al., 1974) when we say, "Don't be depressed," or treat depression as an abnormal experience, which suggests that the experience is a disorder. In a similar vein, William Schofield (1986) described the paradox in which people in contemporary society are encouraged to believe that frustration and anxiety are bad and abnormal and that we have the knowledge and expertise to prevent unhappiness. The fact is (our fact), we are going to be unhappy some of the time. Further, from the perspective we offer here, attempts at prevention of unhappiness as a concept is a pathology of epistemology. The concept of happiness is defined by its opposite identity member, unhappiness. To eliminate one is to deconstruct or eliminate the possibility of either. Again, life happens. We find it interesting that the sentence *Life happens* seems to have replaced *S**t happens* and is applied to less-than-enjoyable human experiences. But *Life happens* can also fit uplifting and joyous human experiences. It can also normalize human experience. It seems that recently more attention is called to the "s**t" that happens rather than the good things. Indeed, it is through the occasional presence (or dream) of good things that other things get punctuated as bad. It is all about values. Paul Dell (1983) noted that therapists do not treat problems; they treat values.

We do not question the well-intentioned efforts of many mental health professionals, but we do question the limits of benevolence when would-be benevolent activities are usurped in the tradition of entrepreneurship and/ or are turned into political issues and economic ventures. We are concerned about the degree to which consumers may take information from competing professional groups who are hawking their wares and think more about their own thinking or feelings and experience more intense feelings about their own feeling, thus creating a "cultural climate of alarm and hypochondria undermining feelings of well-being" (Barsky, 1988, p. 416). What are the appropriate limits for thinking or feeling about one's thoughts and emotions? What are the limits of living consciously or self-consciously? When does such living cease to be living? Are mental health practitioners and researchers part of the problem as they elevate normal malaise about self and relationship to the status of mental illness in need of therapy? Are we, through our good intentions and what are purported to be solutions to problems or proactive activities designed to prevent problems, in fact participating in creating anxiety about anxiety and depression about depression? From the perspective of quantum physics and higher-order cybernetics, the answer is, Indeed we are. We are and cannot not be a part of the system. However, we have created a system of beliefs that suggests that we are not a part of the system and can observe without affecting.

Disconcerting events occur in all lives—loneliness, "languishing," social anxiety, fear, guilt, grief, and so on—and they are a part of life. Again, life happens. But meaning is not implicit in the experience. Rather, the meaning of an event or an experience is relative to the story each person tells themselves about such an event. Unfortunately, however, more and more consumers seem to be internalizing the explanations provided by professionals about the events in their lives rather than allowing for and trusting their own explanations. Too often we abnormalize rather than normalize. And the professional explanations typically pathologize such events rather than normalize the event by viewing it in context. Indeed, when a disconcerting event or experience is viewed in context of relationships and beliefs, one will see normalcy—a view consistent with the systemic paradigm.

For example, for years we have been told that divorced families are broken and that the children of divorce are far more likely to experience problems than are those raised in their intact family of origin. On the one hand, there is very little or contradictory evidence to support these assertions. And on the other hand, to the extent that they are true, how much have our negative predictions influenced negative outcomes. Seeds of concern planted in the fertile minds of very self-conscious people who try to do things the "right way" or consciously not do things the "wrong way" will thrive. Once again, "right way" and "wrong way" reflect values.

Indeed, malaise can be diagnosed and subsequently experienced as mental illness. And if it is given status as mental illness and "treated," then one may develop malaise about one's malaise. The illusion that there is knowledge and expertise to prevent unhappiness is alive and well. It is our belief that this elevation is driven in large, if not full, measure by professional therapists and researchers. Therapists and researchers are not independent observers of the societies to which they belong and whose roles are socially sanctioned. They are active participants in their societies. It is important that they see themselves *in* the society instead of seeing themselves *and* the society (Sarason, 1981). Thus, the professional socially constructed stories will fit the society in which therapists and researchers practice. Any new version of the *DSM* that comes out typically adds new or revised disorders and soon filters into the language of consumers, becoming the presenting problems voiced in therapy. Professionally diagnosed "disorders" thus become part of social discourse as people self-consciously experience themselves, observe, and experience others. The names assigned to disorders becomes the language clients present in their self-diagnoses.

In therapy and in our publications for public consumption, we have enormous power in that the explanations we offer people to understand their lives tend to become their personal explanations and their experience. We provide the language for their experience. Through our choice of explanation, it is in our power to normalize or pathologize events and thus provide either hope or despair. As Schofield (1986) observed, as a function of the criteria by which we make a diagnosis, we can influence the proportion of the population that is defined as either mentally healthy or mentally ill.

Schofield's observation seems consistent with the idea that the concepts of mental health and mental illness as social constructs are relative phenomena. That is, the incidence of mental illness is relative to the rigor of standards developed by professionals to define whether behaviors and experiences shall be relegated to this category. The standards tend to become more "liberal" or more "conservative" (not to be confused with a political connotation) as a function of the number of mental health professionals and resources available (Schofield, 1986). A liberal definition would have more people experiencing themselves as mentally ill or having relationship dysfunction. Conservative definitions would have fewer people having such experiences. Schofield (1986) also points out that any increase in the number of people defined as needing mental health services is followed by an increase in the number of therapists to provide those services. Of course, more therapists need more clients to make a livable income, hence more liberal definitions of mental illness or relationship dysfunction and thus the vicious cycle of supply of therapists creating the demand for services.

In any case, the cultural explanations and values that become peoples' experience of themselves and their relationships are often professional constructions. These constructions also appear in therapist's websites describing and extolling the virtues of their practices. They are the problems we have constructed as the decontextualized phenomena about which people must be concerned and for which help is available. Popular press books that use these professional constructions participate in creating experiences of self and relationships that are often portrayed as ominous. Hospital advertisements hype the curative services available and provide checklists of behaviors and experiences to be aware of that may be indicative of serious problems. Talk-show hosts have guests whose stories may participate in increasing the degree to which people self-consciously observe themselves and others. It seems we feed and find virtue in stories of people who have overcome. And life has a way of providing us with many experiences that we need to "overcome." Living with and through may be another option.

However, when one watches or hears an interview with a victim or a witness to a disaster, often one hears "self-reports," which sound like quotes from professional textbooks. They are akin to the cliché responses that sports heroes give to reporters or that counseling addicts give to their tenth therapist using all the correct buzzwords. Indeed, each day many new problems in need of solution are offered for public consumption. And with each new problem come miracle cures that supposedly not only will solve the problem but also will preclude its reoccurrence. With increasing frequency, clients come for therapy with a self-diagnosis provided by professional and lay authors, talk-show hosts and guests, or a friend's definitions of how they should feel or how their marriage or family should be.

We believe a part of the problem lies in the normative standards developed by research on "normal" or "abnormal" persons, marriages, and families, for each norm or standard becomes a guide against which people measure themselves or their relationships. In effect, we give people new and more sophisticated sets of shoulds by which they measure their personal levels of satisfaction and dissatisfaction. For example, we have encountered many couples who entered marriage so concerned about divorce and so self-consciously trying to live the model that was supposed to preclude divorce that divorce became almost inevitable. One explanation is that the range of "acceptable" behavior designed for and bought into by these couples is so narrow that there is an increased probability that a high percentage of behaviors will fall outside the range of acceptable. Thus, the couple ends up feeling like they have failed and/or blaming each other for not doing what they should have done or been. By contrast, we believe that our normative standards must make room for the unique emotional system that is each person, couple, and family. There must be room for anarchy. There must be room for error. In any relationship, mischief is important. Difference can be a resource—not a problem.

A complicating factor is the fact that consumers, and potentially clients, are socialized into having a great faith in science and technology and believing in the myth of naturalism, which suggests that living, marriaging, and familying should not be trusted to the untrained. Thus, people defer to the wisdom of professionals. We have sold people well on what we call the myth of professionalism: that we professionals have the answers and that consumers should turn their lives over to our knowledge and expertise.

A related area of normal mental health practice that deserves attention is the process of diagnosis and assessment. The concept of diagnosis is consistent with the medical model. The diagnostic process not only transforms the client's story (complaints or problems in living) into a professional construction of the client's problem, but also the professional's conception of the problem is generally viewed as what is really going on in the client system. In formal assessment, the choice of instrument, whether by formal inventory or a clinician's questions, is crucial. The process of assessment shapes the reality experienced by the client. Different instruments and different clinicians' diagnostic questions give clients very different ways of experiencing (storying) themselves. Indeed, the very questions asked by clinicians in the therapy interview participate in defining the way clients experience themselves. Conceptually, the map is not the territory, but the map used by the therapist becomes the territory for clients. Even the websites clinicians use to advertise their wares and services serve to socialize prospective clients into specific deficit or problem categories. The forms clients are required to complete at the outset of their therapy experience (consistent with the medical model) continues the socialization into the medical model and the diagnostic categories consistent with that model. The whole process is a system that is totally consistent within itself. As such, it does not raise questions about itself. A system that is totally consistent within itself does not actually raise questions about itself.

Such power of socialization and transformation has been demonstrated in research in quantum physics, which suggests that the phenomenon under investigation takes the form of the theory underlying the development and application of the instrument (Briggs & Peat, 1984). The evidence from quantum physics reminds us that we cannot just observe; we cannot not participate. Our participation socializes clients into the theory that guides our observations and becomes the reality through which they experience themselves. The diagnostic and therapeutic story of the participant and therapist becomes the story clients use to "understand" themselves. The fact that the story can be useful in helping clients is not in question. Any theory of therapy can be useful—but it is never true with a capital *T*. That shall ever elude us. That which can be therapeutic can also be toxic.

If we assume that the observations and impressions presented in this chapter are plausible, then several implications for therapeutic practice come to mind:

1. We must be aware of the power of our sciences as we develop normative standards that influence how people experience themselves.
2. We must be aware that our normative standards of healthy or unhealthy may be so restrictive that the experience of "normalcy" may be the exception rather than the rule.
3. We must be aware that while consciously trying to live up to a normative standard may be useful to a degree, there may be a point of diminishing returns relative to the well-being experienced by our clients. This is especially crucial if the standard approaches some utopian notion of what life and living is all about or does not fit the unique circumstances that comprise each client system.
4. Just as it is important to have a sensitivity to and respect for cultural, ethnic, and racial differences and be careful about applying normative standards to people without respect for their differences, we must also entertain the possibility that each individual, couple, and family is its own unique culture worthy of the same respect offered the more obvious differences between cultures.
5. It is important that we be client-centered rather than theory-centered: that is, that we listen to the clients and their unique life stories rather than imposing the translation of the life stories as mandated by the theory of the therapist.
6. We may want to help therapists become conscious of and market normative standards with a truth in labeling component that reads something like the following:

This needs survey, checklist, book, intake form, or article is based on a specific theory of people, couples, or families. While this theory may provide a useful way for you to think about yourself, your relationship, or your family, be forewarned that the generic theory may or may not fit you and your unique life situation. Many other theories and models are available to you. Some of the other models may fit you better and be more useful to you. Further, all such models have a limited range of applicability, and any generic model should be viewed as suggestive rather than prescriptive. One of the side effects of applying this or any model to yourself, your relationship, or family is that you may experience as problematic things that you did not know were problems (i.e., they are only problems and values consistent with that point of view). Thus, any solution that is prescribed for you very probably will elicit different problems. A problem-free life is never possible as long as we have values and standards by which we measure ourselves, relationships, and families. Paul Dell (1983) noted that we don't treat problems; we treat values.

Indeed, the current professional therapy context does not encourage people to think for themselves. But even if they did, we are not sure this is even possible. Researchers, therapists, and clients do not think for themselves. Therapists, researchers, and clients are socialized into the concepts of the specific worldview into which they have been socialized without conscious awareness that their worldview is *a* worldview—not *the* worldview. The normative, medical model is a model—not *the* model.

We believe that we can be free only to the extent to which we know how we are controlled. Then perhaps we may experience a measure of freedom—and perhaps compassion and tolerance for those who are controlled by different cultural concepts. We professionals can help people develop a self- and other-consciousness that includes context (i.e., which experience of self or others makes "sense" or is useful), not pathological when viewed in context. Normalizing rather than pathologizing may be more constructively "therapeutic." Of course, viewing experience or behavior in context is inconsistent when decontextualized individuals are the primary unit of analysis. "Normalizing" requires a view of the context of which all of us are a part. With this view, we assess individuals but ignore that we are a part of the context that cannot not affect how the individual is in the context of diagnosis.

Chapter 2

Believing Is Seeing

Exploring the Limits of Knowing

William Blake (BrainyQuote, n.d.) noted, "He who would do good to another must do it in minute particulars. General good is the plea of the scoundrel, hypocrite and flatterer." This quote seems appropriate in this chapter, where we seek to raise consciousness in the service of a "general good." Therefore, we plead guilty to being scoundrels, hypocrites, and flatterers. Indeed, much of what we present borders on sacrilege as we challenge sacred cows in normative social science and mental health practice.

We view ourselves as systems-theory purists. Our philosophical leanings are toward higher-order cybernetics, postmodernism, and social constructivism, and it is this perspective that allows us to see the issues we raise in this chapter. We acknowledge that awareness of these problems is a function of our particular perspective; that is, believing is seeing.

Systems theory is the seminal theory underlying much of the practice of marriage and family therapy (Becvar & Becvar, 2013). It assumes as a fundamental position a totally connected universe in which every thing, person, and creature fits in a logically coherent way. From this perspective, there is no way to stand outside of or just observe the workings of the universe, for that to which we belong has no outside for us. This is higher-order cybernetics. Of course, systems theory is simple and rich, but it necessitates a radical change in thinking about ourselves as social scientists and mental health professionals. As therapists of all professional identities are aware, alternative ways of thinking create dissonance, and the alternative of systems thinking provides no exception to this rule. This chapter explores some of the consequences for normative social science and mental health practice of operating in a manner that is logically consistent with a systemic perspective.

Certainly, systems theory is not consistent with the context of Western ideology and the related political and economic systems of which the mental health professions are an integral part. It is not consistent with the narrative story and traditions of our society, with their focus on autonomy and individual responsibility; a belief that there isn't anything we can't overcome if we work at it hard enough; faith in the ability of science to provide solutions to problems; and a commitment to a work ethic according to which economic success is equated with virtue and failure is seen as moral weakness (Becvar, 1983). Nor is systems theory consistent with the practice of what Kuhn (1970) calls "normal science," which remains strongly wedded to reductionism and substance, as well as to positivistic and postpositivistic epistemological assumptions.

Systems theory has also been accused, and rightly so, of being apolitical, amoral, a-aesthetic, and areligious (Churchman, 1979). It does not espouse a particular social order or arrangement. Causality, if addressed at all, must be understood as reciprocal. According to systems theory, we as researchers cannot just observe. Rather, we become aware that by our observations, we intrude, we perturb, and we transform the phenomena we are attempting to study. Thus, systems theory challenges the validity and perhaps even the morality of the concept of social scientist and mental health practitioner as expert. It suggests that the subjects of our research should participate in developing the theories we use to explain their social and personal experiences. That is, normal science allows us to view ourselves as separate from the phenomena we study and therefore enables us to "discover." Systems theory, by contrast, requires that we include ourselves in the equation and understand that we will "discover" what we *believe* exists "out there." Or as Wilson (1990) writes,

> We cannot make meaningful statements about some assumed "real universe," or some "deep reality" underlying "this universe," or some "true reality" etc., apart from ourselves and our nervous systems and other instruments. Any statements we do make about such a "deep" reality separate from us can never become subject to proof, or to disproof, and that makes them "meaningless" (or "noise"). (p. 173)

Further, the systems perspective does not encourage the search for underlying causes or problems, an integral part of "normal" mental health practice, theory, and research. Systems theory would have us ask what rather than why, which is such an important part of our Western ideology and the tradition of Newtonian physics. It even challenges the concept of "problem" by providing a framework for understanding the logic, fit, or normalcy of all behavior in context. And any phenomenon requires context to have meaning (G. Bateson, 1972). We are reminded, therefore, of the environmental fallacy (Churchman, 1979), of the view that every problem reflects a value perspective (Lather,

1986) that, unless taken into consideration, may not only solve the problem but may also give rise to more serious problems. Systems theory thus suggests that we examine the assumptions and values we punctuate in defining a problem as a problem. It would have us file an environmental-impact statement before any attempted solution is implemented. Thus, systems theory does not address the problems and issues described by various political groups in a way that would satisfy these political groups. In one sense, it is too powerful, and in another sense, it is impotent for immediate resolution of socially defined problems. The political context of research aimed at the resolution of problems demands that the questions and subsequent answers be consistent with the prevailing paradigm. That is, the answers must be politically and psychologically correct.

In addition, our culture separates mind from body—and both from social context. It asks both/and rather than either/or questions. Systems theory provides a unifying perspective that avoids these distinctions and allows us to see mind and body as one, as well as to integrate cognition, affect, and behavior within and between people. Rather than a concept of mind localized within the self (brain), it suggests the possibility of a nonlocal, universal mind. According to Wilson (1990),

> In quantum mechanics, since the 1920s, non-local effects—correlations without connections—have seemed to many physicists the only explanation of some of the behavior of subatomic systems. (Bohr used the word "non-local" as early as 1928.) Bell merely proved mathematically that these non-local effects indeed must exist if quantum math meshes with the observed universe. In these non-local effects, when we say no connection exists to explain the correlation, we mean, more bluntly, that no "cause" exists—in any sense that we have ever understood "cause." (p. 163)

This may describe Gregory Bateson's (1972) pattern, which connects or, as he wrote, "[t]here is a universal mind of which the individual mind is only a subsystem . . . in the total interconnected social system and planetary ecology" (p. 461). Watts (1972) offered a similar view:

> Self, is the whole cosmos as it is centered around the particular time, place and activity called John Doe. Thus, the soul is not in the body, but the body is in the soul, and the soul is the entire network of relationships and processes which make up your environment, and apart from which you are nothing. (pp. 62–63)

Clearly, such conceptions do not fit Western ideology and normative, medical-model therapeutic practice, which values helping people experience a self separate from the context of which it is necessarily a part and separates body from mind in the self.

Western societies also ask that social science researchers provide both certainty and specific solutions to problems. These societies also insist that the "specific solutions" must fit the problems as defined by the ideology of the societies of which social science researchers are a part. Systems theory, once again like the perspective offered by quantum physics, would have us understand that the only certainty is uncertainty (Capra, 1983). That is, "[n]on-Aristotelian logic deals with existential/operational probabilities. Aristotelian logic deals with certainties, and in the lack of certainties throughout most of life, Aristotelian logic subliminally programs us to invent fictitious certainties" (Wilson, 1990, p. 174). However, instead of seeking facts or the true explanation, systems theory and most philosophers of science suggest that "facts" are value and framework relative and that it is quite possible to have contradictory though equally valid facts relative to the value framework of our research and assessment questions (Bartlett, 1983; Lather, 1986).

Further, while paying homage to diversity, our society, in fact, values a certain kind of person, marriage, and family. Thus, normal science practitioners and researchers working within this context follow suit and develop models that "characterize, classify, specialize; they distribute along a scale, around a norm, hierarchize individuals in relation to one another and if necessary, disqualify and invalidate" (Foucault in White & Epston, 1990, p. 74). Accordingly, research data aimed at establishing the characteristics of normal individuals, successful marriages, and functional families becomes the basis for therapeutic assessment and concerted efforts to produce standardized individuals, couples, and families. Indeed, the education of most graduate students in the social sciences includes training in producing such standardized individuals, couples, and families as they learn to use standardized assessment and therapeutic procedures. Or as Hoffman (1990) notes, "Therapists also have their eyes bandaged with texts, although it is easy to be totally unaware that this is the case" (p. 10). The textbooks are generally used to transmit the received-view models of normative social science and mental health practice.

Such models are potentially problematic in a variety of ways. For example, in 1988 we presented a paper on higher-order cybernetics. Following the presentation, a friend heard the following comment from another participant: "That's the trouble with systems theory; you have to think too much." Alfred North Whitehead once noted that the "whole object of science is to avoid thinking as much as possible" (in Bartlett, 1983, p. 11). One way to avoid thinking is by relying on models. Or as Bartlett (1983) has written,

[s]cience can be said to progress relative to the effectiveness of its models. Any model is simplified representation of (usually only some aspect of) reality. Science concerns itself with investigating its own models, their predictive

capabilities, their description and explanatory power, their consistency. When a model shows signs of misfit, when the data do not conform to the expectations of a theory, the model is revised or discarded. (p. 11)

Already this is an admission that we require simplified representations to cope with a complex reality. It is also an admission that we expend our efforts in working on those representations, improving and developing them. We don't confront "reality" head-on. Our models and the mathematical tools we use to develop, analyze, and evaluate them are all in the category of *intellectual crutches*. They serve us precisely because the thought that has been invested in them reduces the amount of subsequent thought required to organize information.

The models we use as "intellectual crutches" tend to be logically consistent with the practice of normal science in the tradition of positivism and postpositivism. Further, most graduate education, indeed most education, is socialization into received-view models according to which students are taught the politically and psychologically correct ways to be a member of a particular profession, complementing the politically and psychologically correct ways for members of that profession to participate in society.

Barsky (1988) has noted a similar phenomenon in the health field, reminding us as well of the mind-body connection in all professions concerned about health. He writes that despite improvements in general health status during the past 20 or 30 years, the individual's sense of their own healthiness has declined. That is, while there has been a substantial increase in the attention that individuals pay to their bodies, to the pursuit of a healthy lifestyle, and to attempts to reduce risk factors, there has been an erosion in the individual's sense of well-being. In other words, the "increasing scrutiny itself amplifies discomfort and dysfunction and results in a more negative appraisal of one's health" (Barsky, 1988, p. 416).

Barsky also points out that the degree to which health has been industrialized and commercialized has added to a general sense of dissatisfaction. The myth that good health can be purchased is phase 2 of a campaign in which we are first warned about possible disease and dangers and the need to take immediate action:

In the process, deep-seated fears about disease are mobilized, and insecurities about health and longevity are intensified. As a result, many come to feel less secure about their health, more worried about the possibility of disease, and more absorbed in trivial symptoms. (Barsky, 1988, p. 416)

A climate of alarm and hypochondria is thereby promulgated by a "medico-media" hype for which not only the media, public relations personnel, advertisers, and manufacturers but also representatives of the health profession share responsibility.

If one considers this position and substitutes mental health and illness and family function and dysfunction for the physical health and disease metaphors, the paradox in the health field of concern to Barsky becomes our concern, as well. And this, we feel, should be the concern of all mental health professionals who are, at some level, concerned about reducing the incidence of mental illness or family dysfunction. The question we raise is, are our efforts at normal mental health practice and normal science in the mental health field paradoxically eroding the sense of well-being that we strive for and seek to enhance?

According to Longino (1990), the philosophy of science follows the science of the day; it does not have an identity of its own. The science of our day may be characterized as a battleground of competing epistemologies reflecting competing ideologies of the society in which research (and therapy) is practiced. Longino (1990) asks, "To what extent do or should scientific theories shape moral and social values? To what extent do social and moral values shape scientific theories?" (pp. 4–5). Indeed, we see what is happening within the field of marriage and family therapy as an example of the current state of the philosophy of science as we ostensibly battle over qualitative versus quantitative methodologies. However, we believe the issues go much deeper. In our view, systems theory as developed in marriage and family therapy has been one bright light in the darkness of the mental health field, allowing the free flow of ideas and encouraging creativity and even what is considered to be craziness, at least when viewed from the perspective of normative mental health practice.

However, in the process of focusing on creating and learning models that describe the way things are or should be, we have instead prevented people from developing an epistemology that has a conscious awareness of itself (G. Bateson, 1972; Keeney, 1983). Further, our models increasingly have tended to restrict the range of freedom for the practice of marriage and family therapy to that which logically fits the models. Thus, today we find ourselves having to classify our clientele in terms that are politically and ideologically acceptable according to the definitions of the mainstream mental health professions, for it is not acceptable to classify our clients as having a marriage or family problem; as having a problem that makes sense given the context within which it emerged; or as having a problem that is a function of attempts to live according to the utopian, contradictory, and/or paradoxical rules generated by the social sciences.

Perhaps what is most distressing is that marriage and family therapists seem to be ignoring not only their roots but also the lessons learned in quantum physics. As Niels Bohr has noted, "It used to be thought that physics describes the universe. Now we know that physics only describes what we can say about the universe" (in Wilson, 1990, p. 69).

In our review of the literature, however, we have become acutely aware of the stranglehold that the political and economic order appears to have on us in their promotion of objective empiricism. Indeed, the concept of science remains relatively unchallenged; it is viewed as a fundamental that by and large is unjudged in terms of its consequences—that science continues its allegiance to reductionism, objectivity, substance, and material. It is a tautology that spins around itself inasmuch as the ecology of ideas that is this science does not include an exploration of the inputs and outputs of its practice and how it maintains itself. And this recursive system-maintaining practice is not unlike the recursive behaviors of individuals, couples, and families who constantly recycle their attempts at solutions, logical within a system that nevertheless remains unchanged.

Many years ago, Fox wrote an article on the politics of research in the United States that continues almost 30 years later. Fox (1990) wrote, "The purposes and methods of any research that influences health policy must be consistent with the values (or more broadly, the ideas . . .) held by the most influential people in American politics at any time" (p. 481). He adds,

> The priorities of research sponsors and journal editors influenced the market, especially its academic sector, for researchers interested in health policy. Jobs in professional schools and social science departments were offered most frequently to people who used the methods of economics, policy analysis, epidemiology, and biostatistics. Responsible teachers reinforced the implications of these events, advising graduate students who could not accept the dominant model of research to try another field. (Fox, 1990, p. 482).

Knowledge that bears on policy, like knowledge about anything else, is made and remade by people in particular political situations; it is, in sociologists' useful metaphor, socially constructed (Gergen, 1991). Unlike people who work in some other areas of inquiry, however, those of us whose research bears on policy cannot, even temporarily, separate ourselves from the political culture (or, if you prefer a different metaphor, the policy system) in which we live. Fox (1990) asserts, "We must endure the irony of studying ourselves at the same time that we solemnly apply our methods of studying what other people have done" (p. 498).

We find this description applicable, as well, to what is happening within our field. At the same time, we recognize the consequences of trying to operate within this field in a way that is inconsistent with the dominant model, for research outside this paradigm may well be perceived as threatening. And perhaps the greatest threat to the current system is that offered by research consistent with the constructivist paradigm:

> From a constructivist paradigmatic position, qualitative research is inextricably bound in the relationship between the researcher and the data. Often, from this perspective, the exploration process is called inquiry rather than research. This serves to note a difference between the concept of research, which implies objectivity, and inquiry, which is subjective in nature. The use of the term *inquiry* also opens up other forms of questioning, different from the traditional scientific method. . . . There is the belief that there are many equally accurate ways to describe events in the social world and it is not possible for any observer(s) to have privileged access to what really happens in the social world by uniformly applying a specific method of observation. (Gale, 1992, pp. 5–6)

However, normal science researchers may view inquiry consistent with the constructivist paradigm as solipsistic, as nihilistic, and as undermining the proper conduct of science. It does not provide empirically based models; inquiry from within this paradigm is a unique event. Knowledge is the product of the union of inquirer and subject of inquiry at that particular time and place. As a unique event, it is not replicable and not generally generalizable. To us, this inquiry is metaphoric of therapy consistent with the social constructionism paradigm, wherein knowledge is viewed as evolving from relationship. Indeed, it is relationship.

In 1938, Whitehead (in Bartlett, 1983) wrote that epistemology is about the study of relationships. Gregory Bateson (1972) described, as a pathology of epistemology, the focus on nouns as real things and concepts as independent, as opposed to seeing relationships. Rather than the subject-object split, inquiry from the constructivist perspective encompasses an organismic, wholistic view, and knowledge is understood as being collaboratively cocreated. One does not stand apart from; one becomes one with one's knowing. Or as noted by Eddington,

> [w]e have found a strange foot-print on the shores of the unknown. We have devised profound theories, one after another, to account for its origin. At last, we have succeeded in reconstructing the creature that made the foot-print. And, lo! It is our own. (in Wilson, 1990, p. 168)

However, it continues today to be a revolution to think in terms of pattern and relationships rather than of substance and material. It is a revolution to see connectedness rather than independence. It is a revolution to challenge the efficacy of technology to answer our most important questions. And certainly, it is a revolution to view knowledge as a social construction that serves political and ideological purposes. Indeed, some might view cybernetics and constructivism as a return to the medieval mysticism that normal science in its evolution sought to overcome.

Many clients must overcome what Gregory Bateson (1972) described as pathologies of epistemology in order to find solutions for their problems. We believe that all mental health professionals face a similar challenge if we and the society of which we are a part are to experience meaningful change, for we believe that assuming we can know what is best for someone else is a moral issue. And truth in labeling would require us to publicly acknowledge both the limits of our knowledge and an awareness that believing is seeing.

Chapter 3

Before the Beginning

This chapter continues therapy on the concepts and practices of therapy that involve helping the reader/therapist/theorist develop an epistemology that has a conscious awareness of itself. Systems theory (cybernetics), particularly at the level of second-order cybernetics, would thus have therapists become self-consciously aware of observing themselves participating in "treating" and constructing the problems that clients present when they seek therapy. Thus, systems theory is about relationships and stories that always include you—both as the observer and participant in that which is being observed. You the professional are a part of your clients' lives before they seek therapy. Thus, as clients' social discourse includes mental health practitioners and *DSM* discourse, you are in their lives before the beginning of therapy. Indeed, where in this world can you be and not be a part of it and influence it by your participation. You as a mental health practitioner are *in* the society, not an objective observer outside the society.

How can there be something before the beginning? That is an easy question to answer: Beginnings and endings are conceptually joined together. In life there are no time-outs. In life the punctuation of a beginning or ending is arbitrary in that an ending may also be seen as a beginning. For the purposes of this chapter, we take the position that the problems people bring to therapy evolve in the time and space before they present themselves or are presented for therapy. In addition, the role of the therapist is in place waiting to be activated when people experience problems in living. That said, let's go "back to the beginning."

In the movie *The Sound of Music*, the nanny (Julie Andrews) begins a song with the children something like this: "Let's start at the very beginning, a very good place to start. When you read, you begin with A, B, C; when you sing, you begin with do, re, mi." Her words are the preface to the famous song many of you know. Amazingly, she and the children launch into a song in perfect harmony without any rehearsal (smile). The following is our story of "before the beginning" of therapy. The process has had a long rehearsal.

We believe that therapists might find it useful to have a story about how their clients become clients with their specific problems and how these problems are logically consistent with the worldview or Weltanschauung of their societies. It is our story that the therapy relationship is shaped well before therapist and client meet in formal session. Many events and experiences for both clients and therapists are required and precede the formal ritual or process called therapy, all of which shape the form of therapy and the expectations of both clients and therapists. This chapter describes some of these preliminary events and experiences—our A, B, C and do, re, mi. Be assured that we do not expect you to launch into song at the end of the chapter. However, feel free to do so. Groaning is okay, as well.

One of the basic preliminary requirements for therapy is that people must experience "problems" or have "complaints" about their lives, their relationships, or both and that they bring these to the therapy experience or other people in their lives suggest to them that they have problems in need of therapy. In some form, they experience "problems in living." Sometimes the problems may be referred to formally as "disorders" that need to be "treated" and/or problems in living with others and/or themselves that need a solution, known by more colloquial or in layman's language, "Life sucks," "I'm just not happy," "My marriage is failing," "Fix my kid," and so on. Or they may come with a self-diagnosis derived from the disorders set forth in the *DSM*. Or sometimes they just "wonder" about life, its meaning and purpose.

So where do these problems come from? How do they believe their lives and relationships should be or should not be? And how do these problems get assigned a metaphor (diagnosis)? Our answer to these questions is both simple and complicated (of course). We shall try to make things as simple as possible but no simpler. Here is a story—with a preliminary amendment. While there is a possibility of historical, genetic, or so-called hereditary components in the background of behavior, such factors are not independently observable except in cases of severe mental or physical deficiency. We offer this amendment to our general assumption that problems in living evolve in relationships. We make several assumptions.

Our first assumption is that there are no problems floating around in space. Further, problems and challenges are not spontaneously generated within the person. They evolve and become a natural part of human experience by virtue of living in a society or culture. They evolve in relationships and are maintained in relationships. They are not "caused." The names for these problems come from the professional and popular social constructions as language in the society. Indeed, professional language becomes part of social discourse very quickly. Popular media does its job well by broadcasting the more recently elected disorders to its audience. Thus, as phenomena that evolve as a natural part of the social context, the problems clients bring to the therapy room are not anomalies in the same sense that physical disease is not an anomaly when viewed in the context of the etiology of the disease. Indeed, the social context and its language designate the problems people experience and are presented as reasons to seek therapy. Some people who are referred for therapy may not even experience a problem but are following a suggestion from their social network that suggests they have a problem. And some people are mandated by courts to seek therapy, whether they experience problems in need of therapy or not.

This last point suggests that most of the problems people present in therapy evolve in relationships. Indeed, other people may have a problem with the other person and suggest that they receive therapy. Of course, from this one might wonder who "really" has the problem—the observer or the observed— or are they really different? Further, people in different social and cultural contexts may experience different problems in need of therapy, although this is changing somewhat as Western ideologies and *DSM* diagnostic categories and treatment protocols get exported to other countries and cultures.

These social contexts cannot not affect the biology of people; "mind," body, and social context are connected—cannot not be. Therapeutic contexts (we choose not to use the term *treatment* or *intervention*), even those that focus only on either mind, body, or social context, cannot not affect the others. Mind, body, and social contexts are invented categories. They are our constructed distinctions—useful for some purposes but of doubtful or limited utility for other purposes. Gregory Bateson (1972) and Douglas Flemons (1991) noted that the first act of knowing is to create a distinction, but the world in which we live is never actually divided. These distinctions exist only in our models, and all models are but "models"—none of them describe the territory and have a limited range of applicability or utility.

A second assumption is that these problems or challenges reflect the values and expected personal and social behavior that are a necessary part of any society. There is a social paradigm—a collective consciousness. All societies evolve rules for living that serve as guides for "right" living, and social control mechanisms for enforcement are part of the scenario. This overarching set of rules for living are embedded in what is called a Weltanschauung or worldview. Societies also evolve visions of a life that is fulfilling and satisfying, which reciprocally imply or explicitly state behavior and experiences that are viewed as problematic. Everything valued has a flip side, something that is not valued.

The relative frequency and severity of problems or challenges experienced depends on how much latitude the society allows before a behavior or experience exceeds the parameters of acceptable experience or behavior. Criteria for definitions of "mental illness" can be liberal or conservative (Schofield, 1986). Moreover, the parameters of acceptable behavior can vary greatly in different circumstances.

In effect, problems, experienced or ascribed, may be viewed as violations of the social paradigm. The narrower the range of acceptable behavior or experience allowed by a society, the more people will be judged or judge themselves to be in violation of the rules. We refer the reader to Schofield's (1986) observation about conservative and liberal definitions of mental illness. In general, diagnostic terms, violations of a social paradigm are broadly referred to as "mad" (crazy) or "bad" (criminal). Sometimes these metaphors are combined; that is, sometimes people are bad because they are mad.

Now we explicate the concept of a Weltanschauung or worldview into which people are socialized. The socialization occurs without conscious awareness that they are being socialized into a Weltanschauung or worldview—one of many worldviews in our world. It is our story that Weltanschauungs and worldviews contain the "thou shalls" and the "thou shall nots"—with the emphasis on the "thou shall nots." These may be explicit, as in laws or commandments, or implicit in the form of common practice. So let's begin again. (So many beginnings. One wonders when will beginnings end. They will, and they won't; beginnings and endings are ever united conceptually.)

According to Gergen (1991), Pearce (1988), and Watts (1972), any person born to a society or culture is socialized into the worldview, paradigm, or narrative story of that culture or society. This worldview is embedded in the language of the culture or society. Sarason (1981) describes the socialization process as follows:

> One does not choose to have a Weltanschauung. It emerges and develops over a lifetime. It may change in certain respects but rarely in regard to its origins and bases, which remain silent and axiomatic. One's Weltanschauung is more than knowledge and less than language. What one calls knowledge is largely a consequence of Weltanschauung and not its cause. The knowledge one receives from others, and the way one receives and organizes such knowledge, reflects a view of man and the world. The infant and young child are unaware of this process but those responsible for rearing the child are quite aware that they are inculcating a way of viewing self and the world. But they, like the child, are unaware of how much of what they are trying to do bears the imprint of a particular Weltanschauung. (p. 46)

Pearce (1988) tells the story about the acquisition of a worldview differently:

> A social worldview, one shared with other people, is structured in our infant minds by the impingements on us from, and the verifying responses to us by,

other people. A mind finds its definition of itself not by confrontation with things so much as other minds. We are shaped by each other. We adjust not to the reality of a world, but to the reality of other thinkers. When we have finally persuaded and/or badgered our children into "looking objectively" at their situation, taking into consideration those things other to themselves, we relax since they are being realistic. What we mean is that they have finally begun to mirror our commitments, verify our life investments, and strengthen and preserve the cosmic egg of our culture. (p. 48)

Alan Watts (1972) makes the same point in a different way:

Our most private thoughts and emotions are not actually our own. For we think in terms of languages and images which we did not invent, but which were given to us by our society. Our social environment has this power just because we do not exist apart from a society. Society is our extended mind and body. (p. 64)

Thus, the society or culture into which we are born and raised provides us with stories. Mair (1988) describes these stories as follows:

Stories are habitations. We live in and through stories. They conjure worlds. We do not know the world other than as story world. Stories inform life. They hold us together and keep us apart. We inhabit the great stories of our culture. We live through stories. We are lived by the stories of our race and place. It is this enveloping and constituting function of stories that is especially important to sense more fully. We are, each of us, locations where the stories of our place and time become partially tellable. (p. 127)

We believe it is important for therapists to have a conscious awareness of the concept of Weltanschauung and the ecology of ideas and stories. Also, it is important that therapists realize that the concept of problem implies values. The concept of value implies something that is preferred in contrast to something that is not preferred. These preferences are a part of the client's Weltanschauung. People who have different values from a different Weltanschauung would not experience the same event as a problem. Weltanschauungs are social constructions that are experienced by people as the way things really are (Becvar & Becvar, 2013). It does make a difference if one believes a Weltanschauung is socially constructed or describes the way the world really is. Indeed, one might say that one is only free to the extent to which one knows how one is controlled by the stories that have been socialized into us without conscious awareness that they are stories and not the way the world really is. Sarason (1972) noted that we are prisoners of our cultures. We believe that this perspective is very important, as it provides a perspective on problems, solutions, and the concept of therapy. Wilson (1986) made the following observation about the stories that are socialized into us:

> To the extent that we remain conscious of this process of superimposing struc-
> ture we will behave liberally and will continue learning throughout life. To the
> extent to which we become unconscious of this process, we will behave funda-
> mentalistically or idolatrously and will never again learn anything after the hour
> at which we (usually unconsciously) elevate a generalization into a dogma and
> stop thinking. (p. 17)

Thus, if you believe that the ideas, concepts, or constructs are socially
constructed rather than describing the real phenomena, then options become
available to you. Your previous ideas can be deconstructed (if they are not
serving you well), and new (and perhaps more useful) ideas can be adopted,
adapted, or constructed. However, if you believe that the ideas, concepts,
or constructs describe the way things really are, then you have few or no
options, and these options typically reflect either/or dichotomous thinking.
Having said this, social constructionism does not deny that events really happen, but a generic meaning ascribed to an event is a function of the Weltanschauung of the society. Basically, a Weltanschauung is a set of standardized
stories (a collective consciousness) that give meaning to events that occur or
are experienced. Individuals within the society may have (and very probably
do have) a different meaning (personal constructs) from the standardized
Weltanschauung of the society (social constructionism). Thus, each person
constructs their own meaning, which may differ from the socially constructed
meaning preferred by the society.

In brief, we doubt that any two people ever give the same meaning to an
experience. In this and in many senses, we are strangers (M. C. Bateson,
2001). We are, each of us, unique emotional and conceptional systems. That
is the one thing all people have in common. We get ahead of ourselves, but
it is important to understand the importance of seeing people and clients as
unique emotional systems. This is one reason that standardized "treatments"
for standardized descriptions (diagnoses) of problems require standardization of people. Thus, standardization (fitting people into categories) loses the
uniqueness that is each person—again, standardized diagnoses and standardized treatments for standardized individuals. Each of us is unique—just like
everybody else.

Again, a Weltanschauung necessarily reflects the values of the society. To
us a society's socially constructed stories refer only to the meaning ascribed
to events. Events really do happen. Thus, the Holocaust really happened, but
the Nazis had one story about it, and fortunately the rest of the world had
another story about it. To justify the Holocaust, the Nazis created different
distinctions from those previously held by the German people. They distinguished people of the Aryan race (although Aryan is not a race) from the Jews
and other fringe groups, who were viewed as inferior and were dehumanized.

In a similar way, Black Africans were construed as less than human by White people, which justified the practice of slavery. Chinese people were construed as less than human but useful as laborers. The social constructions that give meaning to our experiences reflect constructed distinctions based on values, serve practical ends, and maintain the social structures and classes valued by the dominant groups in a society.

Okay then, so what's the problem? Try this. Again, there are no problems floating around in space. The designers of the rules for living in our societies have ingeniously created rules and processes for living, with contradictions and paradoxes that increase the probability that most people will experience themselves, their relationships, and others as crazy to greater or lesser degrees. This may not have been their intent, but these rules are so replete with paradoxes and contradictions that trying to find logic and trying to follow the rules of the society cannot not drive one crazy. Thus, don't wonder why people go crazy; wonder why they do not.

And then there are the problems of people living with each other. Each member of a relationship may view the behavior as problematic if it interferes with the way they want to be. Be the way I want you to be so I can be the way I want to be: Go to therapy and get fixed, unload your baggage, or get your act together. When both people say this to each other, two new clients hit the market, or perhaps, if viewed systemically, the couple will go to therapy.

While we recognize that animals may think, love, plan, grieve, scheme, play, feel pain and joy, and more, the animals in the wild don't seem to have the psychological and relationship problems that we experience. Even in the context of competition with other animals, there is a higher-order cooperation that preserves the necessary balance for the survival of a species to fit ecological contexts. Again, this does not mean that animals don't have emotions; they feel, they have what we would call loyalty, they grieve, they protect their young, and so on. (They may even have self-consciousness, but our worldviews seem to reserve that for the human species.) However, the process of domestication of these creatures often does produce craziness. (Cats may be an exception to this assertion.) Indeed, being socialized into a society can be usefully viewed as a form of domestication.

Once again, every society and culture has a Weltanschauung or worldview that governs the lives of people living in the culture or society. One might also say that a society or culture is its Weltanschauung. Gregory Bateson (1972) noted that we relate to ideas or our conceptions and not things. It contains the correct values, ideals, ideas, goals, and actions required for "citizenship" in that culture or society. It finds its expression in language (i.e., set forth in written rules for living). Mostly, it is unarticulated, and people may be unaware of the standards for living implicit in it until a violation of a standard is experienced. Indeed, one may have no conscious awareness of a rule until it is violated. This reminds us of a cartoon script we recall: A supervisor advises an employee, "It is an unwritten rule that there shall be no written rules." And when a violation is observed, society has institutions and procedures in place to correct violations, which get activated.

What we write next is kind of an aside from what we have written earlier. We have referred to the concepts of society *and* culture. For the purpose of this chapter, we choose to punctuate a society as an overarching context, while culture is a subgroup of a larger society. That seems to be consistent with the arrangements of many civilizations. However, there are some societies where culture and society are identical or nearly so. That is, the overarching paradigm of the society includes only one culture. This seems to be a concept that fits societies that are also theocracies. We believe distinguishing between culture and society is important in that while there may be a Weltanschauung or worldview of a society, a culture in that society may have a different Weltanschauung that governs the lives of its members. This distinction becomes important in that violations of the societal paradigm may not be violations of the cultural paradigm of which the violator is a member. And of course, violations of a cultural paradigm may not be violations of the societal paradigm. Indeed, it may well be that living in a society that includes only one culture would be much easier because there is more consistency. That said, we suspect that even in societies of one culture, there may be differences in subsystems, perhaps the family or a slightly different sect or interpretation of the religion. We return to this topic later, but for now, we continue our story from the previous paragraph.

When a violation is observed, the institutions the society has developed to correct violations are activated. These institutions include police officers, social workers, and therapists. Rainwater (1967) refers to the people in these roles as the "dirty workers." It is important to note that the rules of the broader society take precedence over the rules of subcultures. In any society, there are ranked groups based on a variety of factors (economic, education, religion, social status, etc.). These rules in the Weltanschauung are developed by the highest-ranked groups of the society. Members of subordinate groups or cultures are expected to defer to the rules of the highest-ranked group. Becker (1967) describes the process:

> In any system of ranked-groups, participants take it as given that members of the highest group have the right to define the way things really are. . . . From the point of view of the well-socialized participant in the system, any tale told by those at the top intrinsically deserves to be regarded as the most credible account available. . . . And since . . . matters of rank and status are contained in the mores, the belief has moral quality. We are, if we are proper members of the group, morally bound to accept the definitions imposed on the reality by

the superordinate group in preference to the definitions espoused by subordi-
nates. . . . By refusing to accept the hierarchy of credibility, we express disre-
spect for the entire established order. (p. 241)

Becker's observation is of great importance for you as therapists because
your role is a socially sanctioned, licensed, accredited role within society.
Further, your role serves the society, and "knowledge" that comprises the
conceptual framework that guides your professional practice must logically
complement the Weltanschauung of the society. While the idea is somewhat
controversial, knowledge is not value free. It is our belief that any form of
therapy involving diagnosing problems in living is political. Therapy necessarily is about ethics, politics, and economics. One author (unknown to us) wrote,

I helped a few learn how to modify their behavior so they could stay
out of trouble. I made very little effort to alter the oppressive environment
of the "prison" itself." [This is a necessary consequence of locating the
problem as a disorder within the client and is consistent with contemporary
therapeutic practice.]

It goes beyond merely encouraging the individual to recognize and deal
with environmental stress in his life.

Every encounter with any psychotherapist has political implications.
The psychotherapist either encourages the patient to change existing distri-
butions of power or encourages the patient to accept them.

By reinforcing the positions of those who hold power, the psychotherapist is committing a political act whether he intends to or not. Once this
fact is appreciated, the psychotherapist's search for political neutrality
begins to appear illusory. (Author unknown, in R. Becvar, undated notes
to himself)

Our current sociopolitical climate is as charged as it has ever been—in terms
of the polarization of people around issues on which politicians build their
platforms. Gay marriage. Abortion. Transgender people. Immigrants. Race.
And the list goes on. Emotions are involved, and opinions are strong—and of
course relationships are affected. Remember that every problem we experience
in life reflects a polarized position. We cannot know "up" without experiencing
"down." If you punctuate some things as "beautiful," then other things become
"ugly." If we value one thing, then we are saying the other thing is a problem.
Any distinction that is based on a value necessarily creates that which is valued
and that which is problematic. The number of current "issues" around which

people are rallying come from the distinctions we create, and it is these distinctions that are creating the problems. As a point of comparison, if we were to look at Chinese history and Taoist thought, which began in the Age of Perfect Virtue, the concept of being a part of or one with nature was not a concept because not being a part of nature was inconceivable; that is, it was not conceived. Indeed, there probably were fewer conceptions or distinctions, for the Taoist view of the world was that of an undivided whole. Without the concept of whole, the concept of parts cannot exist. But we digress—but do we?

Okay then, so maybe you as a therapist are getting a sense of the importance of the concept of a worldview and the concepts and values implicit in each worldview. It is now time for another aside that to us logically fits the story we tell. We need to touch again on systems theory (cybernetics). We treat the metaphors systems and cybernetics as similar in meaning. Now, a basic premise of the systems perspective (much more on this to come later) is that all creatures (people included) and things are interconnected. In essence, there is only one system—the cosmos. We punctuate subsystems of the cosmos for our practical purposes in our attempts to "know." Gregory Bateson (1972) noted that the first act of knowing is to create distinctions, which necessarily requires breaking the whole into parts (subsystems). We believe it is important that you "know" that the way you know (epistemology) requires creating distinctions in a world that is never actually divided. Also, in our attempts to "know" (generate knowledge), the distinctions we make reflect the values and the purposes of the research and the society. In the process, scientists typically punctuate themselves as independent observers of the phenomenon they have isolated from the whole for study. They punctuate themselves outside the system they are observing. However, it seems the phenomena elected for study reflect the values of the society of which the scientist is a part. This is particularly true of social scientists (and therapists) who live and work within the Weltanschauung of the society. They are part of the system, not independent observers of the system.

Let's visit Seymour Sarason (1981) once again. He makes a very important observation which is consistent with the systems perspective. He refers to psychologists, but it can apply to all social scientists and therapists. He notes that psychologists often view themselves (outside observers of) *and* the society rather than see themselves and their role (making observations while being a part of) *in* the society. In essence the role of all social scientists who work within the worldview of a society have their roles legally and socially sanctioned by the society. These roles, as socially and legally sanctioned, must logically complement and reflect the values implicit in the worldview of the society of which they are necessarily a part. Accreditation of programs and licensure of graduates of accredited programs provide some assurance that these graduates' roles will reflect the values of the society of which they are a part—indeed, cannot not be a part of it. And yet in our attempts to "know" and do "therapy," we punctuate ourselves as independent observers of society. But our observations reflect the received view or values of the society of which we are a part. We are caught in a fundamental dilemma in our attempts to know, and what you are reading reflects this dilemma. Again, where in this world can you be and not be a part of it? Watts (1972) described a birth of a child as not coming "into" the world but coming "from" or out of the world. That to which you necessarily belong has no outside for you. There is no outside—except as punctuated for pragmatic purposes and select values.

This dilemma reflects the difference between first- and second-order cybernetics (systems). First-order cybernetics asserts that all creatures (including people) and things are interconnected. As mentioned previously, there is only one system—the cosmos. This assertion is made by punctuating oneself making this observation outside the system. Second-order cybernetics would agree with this but would insist on internal consistency. To be internally consistent, observers must include themselves as part of the system being observed. Again, that to which you necessarily belong has no outside for you. And so observers observe themselves as being a part of the system they are observing. Confusing, yes indeed. Important, yes indeed. Thus, the observer (therapist) is both inside and outside—is both participant and observer. Read on.

We believe it is vital that therapists and all people have a worldview in which they view themselves as a part of the system and not independent observers of the system. Their observations are not from a position outside the system. Thus, the process of observation cannot not affect the system. They would live somewhat self-consciously in that they are aware of the worldviews into which they have been socialized. They would also be self-conscious of the systems perspective in that they would see themselves as a part of all systems—not an independent observer of the systems. Thus, they would have a self-conscious awareness of themselves as observers observing their participation in all systems. They would have a worldview that would include an epistemology that has a conscious awareness of itself. Thus, they would know how they know and how what they know became "knowledge." They would have a view that suggests that they participate in creating the problems they are subsequently sanctioned to "treat" by the values implicit in the categories used in diagnosis.

A more liberal definition of mental illness or relationship dysfunction includes more clients to be in "need" of therapy. A more conservative definition expands the range of normalcy in professional literature, which filters into normal discourse—and provides fewer clients. The nature of the problem and the severity of the problem diagnosed depends on how wide or how narrow the range of normalcy used for judging mental illness. In a conservative definition of normalcy, a wider range of behavior is acceptable—more error is

allowed before alarms are rung. From this frame of reference, any announce-
ment of an increase in the number of people with mental illness suggests that
the range of normalcy has become very narrow. One might envision this via
the statistical normal curve. To what degree do we normalize or abnormalize
human experience?

In addition, do we consider context when we assess people in need of
therapy and see their problems as normal experiences in the context (relationships) in which they live? The prevailing map for diagnosis consistent with
the term *mental illness* locates the problem within the person—consistent
with Western ideologies and worldviews. This stands in stark contrast to
therapists who observe via the systems paradigm. They would see the client system in context. When viewing "symptomatic" behavior in context,
the therapists/observers will see normalcy. Moreover, from the perspective
of second-order cybernetics, they would know that whatever story they as
participant-observers use in therapy will become the "reality" or lens through
which the clients begins to see and language themselves. A systems-oriented
therapist would normalize "disorder" or "dysfunction." A medical-model
therapist would treat "disorder" or "dysfunction."

Thus, the professional constructions (lists of symptoms designating disorders), like those in the socially constructed *DSM*, become the constructions client systems use in self-diagnosis as well as in the process of therapy. Indeed,
the map is not the territory, but the concepts and constructs of the map become
the reality that brings clients to therapy, and the map used by the therapist in
therapy becomes the reality for the clients. Social constructions become "real."

And these social constructions are used as people diagnose their own experience: "Am I crazy." These social constructions are used as people observe
and diagnose each other: "It has been over a year, and you are still grieving.
You may have a 'prolonged grief disorder.'" Or seemingly less authoritarian
but equally significant: "You didn't breastfeed your baby!?" or "You have
separate bank accounts!?" or "Stop worrying." (The latter is a "be spontaneous" paradox and is quite successful in producing craziness.) Observations,
questions, and statements like these imply values prescriptions of what a
person should to do or feel and what they should not. These questions and
observations are part of standard social discourse and cannot not produce
self-conscious exploration of one's behavior and experience.

Indeed, members of any society monitor each other's behavior for adher-
ence to "normal" social protocols. In a sense, *normal* implies the "right" way
to be. This, of course, the values implicit in social monitoring, soon become
the values people use to monitor their own behaviors and experiences: "What
is wrong with me? I should be able to stop worrying, but when I try not to
worry, I fail and seem to worry more—and moreover, I worry about my
inability to stop worrying."

So how do people get the problems that they present for therapy? We believe they evolve by participating in a society and by trying to live up to standards that are utopian, paradoxical, and contradictory. These standards are augmented and echoed by the theories of the social sciences and the theories used by credentialed therapists who represent the societies in which they work.

To review the latter, we suggest you go online and read the websites of practicing therapists who list the problems they treat and their areas of expertise. They may vary somewhat from therapist to therapist, but the lists are quite comprehensive. Prospective clients may read the list and pick a term that fits problems they experience and stories their experiences. Other stories are possible, but the language of deficit and dysfunction has gotten much larger. The language of deficit and dysfunction surrounds us—how could we not experience an increase in the number of people defined as and experience themselves as "mentally ill"? The context is a perfect storm for continuing to expand. And as more clients seek therapy, there is a demand for more therapists. This is accompanied by more precise distinctions of deficit and dysfunction in an attempt to meet the need (Schofield, 1986). And of course, an increase in the number of therapists typically means an increase in the number of clients: Supply creates its own demand.

Indeed, the new "normal" involves being in therapy. It has become more socially approved. "You aren't in therapy? What is wrong with you?" Being in therapy seems to have become a litmus test for people to evaluate each other. Indeed, it may take many years of therapy to overcome the effects of a perfect childhood. Then one may become "normal" like the rest of us.

Is there a solution to this escalation of mental illness? We believe there is, but it will not involve doing more of the same that is not working. As mentioned in Chapter 1, our attempted solutions have not only not solved the problem but also have participated in making it worse. A first step would be for social science and therapy theorists and practicing therapists to do therapy on the concepts and constructs currently in use. For a partial, if not the most significant, "cause" of the problem, we professionals need to look in a mirror. Indeed, one of our purposes in writing and sharing our ideas in this book is to help therapists have an epistemology that has a conscious awareness of itself—and to help clients do the same. This may involve doing therapy on the collective consciousness of the worldviews that provide rules for living. Indeed, we may be the only species that needs to articulate rules for living and for living with one another. The more "civilized" we become (read "separate ourselves from nature"), the more precise and encompassing rules we seem to need to choreograph our dance to music whose tempo is getting ever faster.

Chapter 4

Contributions from Social Science and Mental Health Professionals

Social scientists and mental health professionals are representatives of and represent the views of the dominant groups of the society. Stated differently, the subject matter that constitutes the education of social scientists and mental health professionals is consistent with the values of the society of which they are a part. The problems on which they conduct research and treat are those defined as problems by the Weltanschauung of the society.

Schofield (1986) noted that an increase in the number of therapists leads to a subsequent increase in the number of clients, which in turn may be used as an argument for an increase in the number of therapists. This cycle did not serve to alleviate the problem or reduce the incidence of mental illness in the past. However, it did result in an increase of the client population and thus of the professionals to serve them. As Becvar et al. wrote in 1982:

> The identification of a particular group labeled "disabled" or "dysfunctional" by some standard often leads to the creation of a formal agency and a new body of professionals to help that group. At its inception, each such agency has as its ultimate goal the elimination of a need for its services through intervention in the group. Since in the cases of marriages and families, there are always new members of the group, this goal cannot be realized. Thus, the agency and/or professionals tend to maintain both themselves and the target group at which their help is aimed. This is justified if the problem is a result of the nature of the target group. (p. 387)

However, if the agency or professionals maintain themselves by continually focusing on the same individuals or members of that group or if they relax the criteria by means of which phenomena are judged to be dysfunctional, then they are serving only themselves. A reduction of services for a "disabled" group becomes more difficult with the passage of time, for society narrows its range of accommodation as soon as an agency is formed. Persons labeled "disabled" or "dysfunctional" get channeled to its facilities. Those who serve clients through the agency soon develop a vested interest in the maintenance of the agency and the group it serves. And the range of those served may then be controlled by the ability to serve rather than by the need for such services. As the number of professionals increases, there is a greater vested interest in liberalizing the definitions of *mental illness* and, in the case of marriages and families, *pathology*. Schofield (1986) addressed this issue:

> In essence, there is a problem of a reverse approach to diagnosis: we may define as mentally ill any person who does not have perfect mental health, and we may define perfect mental health in terms of such rigorous standards that it is a condition notable for its absence rather than its presence in a majority of the population at a given time. (p. 12)

According to Schofield, the liberalization of the definitions of *mental health* and *pathology* in a system has reached the stage where any unhappiness or a failure to be free of anxiety fall into these categories. In our attempt to help, we may have given the impression, either inadvertently or not, that cures for individual, marriage, and family "pathologies" of unhappiness or the failure to be free of anxiety are known and that treatments are available. Schofield (1986) explained,

> What has changed is man's relative freedom to think about his condition, to be anxious about his anxiety, and to live in a cultural epoch which entertains the thesis that personal frustration of any sort is abnormal, that avoidance of anxiety should be a primary personal goal and that society can provide both the knowledge and the experts for the successful prevention of unhappiness. (p. 44)

A similar idea was suggested by Barsky (1988) in the article "The Paradox of Health," which appeared in the *New England Journal of Medicine*. We discussed this in chapter 3. Barsky describes an issue in biomedicine similar to one we see in the mental health field. Although not specifically addressed, the article also makes us aware of the mind-body connection in all professions concerned about health. Thus, Barsky notes that despite improvements in health status during the past 20 or 30 years, people's sense of their own healthiness has declined. That is, while there has been a substantial increase in attention paid to one's body and the pursuit of a healthy lifestyle, with concomitant attempts to reduce risk factors, there has been an erosion in the individual's sense of well-being. In other words, "This increasing scrutiny, itself amplifies discomfort and dysfunction and results in a more negative appraisal of one's health" (Barsky, 1988, p. 416).

Barsky also points out that the degree to which health has been industrialized and commercialized and has added to a general sense of dissatisfaction. The myth that good health can be purchased is Phase 2 of a campaign in which we are first warned about possible diseases and dangers and the need to take immediate action:

> In the process, deep-seated fears about disease are mobilized, and insecurities about health and longevity are intensified. As a result, many come to feel less secure about their health, more worried about the possibility of disease, and more absorbed in trivial symptoms.
>
> A climate of alarm and hypochondria is thereby promulgated by a "medico-media hype" for which not only the media, public relations, advertisers, and manufacturers but also representatives of the health professions, share responsibility. In such a climate one's sense of well-being is undermined. Indeed, it is harder to feel confident about one's health when sensations and dysfunctions one had assumed to be trivial are portrayed as ominous, the herald of some heretofore unrecognized and undiagnosed disease. Feelings of ill health and disability are amplified when every ache is thought to merit medical attention, every twinge may be the prodrome of a malignant disease, when we are told that every mole and wrinkle deserves surgery. (Barsky, 1988, pp. 416–417)

If one considers this position and substitutes mental health or illness terms for the physical health or disease terms, then the paradox in the health field of concern to Barsky becomes our concern, one we feel should be the concern of all consumers, social scientists, and mental health professionals. Paradoxically, such efforts may be eroding the sense of well-being they intend to enhance.

In essence, we believe that physical symptoms and emotional and relationship malaise do not necessarily fit the concept of mental illness. Rather, the problem may be that of attempted solutions where no problems exist (Wátzlawick et al., 1974). Moreover, the malaise itself may be a product of a finely honed sensitivity to one's experience of self and one's relationships that professionals have encouraged. That is, as we "story" or give people explanations about symptoms or emotional or relationship issues, our explanations can serve to create higher-order problems by oversensitizing them to the pains and struggles of normal life experiences and fostering the belief that "personal frustration of any sort is abnormal, that avoidance of anxiety should be a primary personal goal and that society can provide both the knowledge and the experts for the successful prevention of unhappiness" (Schofield, 1986, p. 44).

In other words, as Virginia Satir (1967) noted, it is not our feelings that are the problem but our feelings about our feelings, for the kind of feelings we have about our feelings is relative to the story we tell ourselves about our feelings. Many questions come to mind at this point. What is the difference that makes a difference (G. Bateson, 1972) between doing good and doing no harm? What are the limits of benevolence when benevolence has been usurped in the tradition of American entrepreneurship and turned into political issues and economic ventures? To what degree do consumers take information from competing professional groups who are hawking their wares and think more about their own thinking and have more intense feelings about their own feelings, thus creating a "cultural climate of alarm and hypochondria, undermining feelings of well-being" (Barsky, 1988, p. 416). At what point does living self-consciously cease to be living?

Life will never be without problems, many of which may seem insoluble. Indeed, life can be experienced as just one damned thing after another. However, given our belief that we construct our reality (Segal, 1986), it behooves us to invent different meanings and value systems from which may emerge different problems that are capable of solution. This means that we must think about and include ourselves in our deliberations. That is, although events certainly occur in our lives, meaning is not implicit in the event; the meaning of an event is relative to the story we tell ourselves about the event. What concerns us is that more and more consumers are telling themselves stories provided by professionals about events in their lives and that such stories increasingly tend to pathologize these events.

Indeed, the process of psychological or marriage and family diagnosis is a search for pathology or deficit. Gergen (1991) notes that the "vocabulary of human deficit has undergone enormous expansion within the present century" (p. 13). He attributes this expansion to the "scientizing" of human behavior as we attempt to generate explanations of undesirable behavior. He notes, "As people acquire the vocabulary, they also come to see self and others in these terms" (p. 15).

Recalling Barsky (1988), the "increased scrutiny" using deficit terminology "amplifies discomfort and dysfunction and results in a more negative appraisal of one's health" (p. 416). Along these same lines, in their review of the literature, Boisvert and Faust (2002) note the following:

[I]atrogenic symptoms may originate from a pathology-oriented belief system through which therapists interpret, reinterpret, or label clients' personal characteristics, life script or distress. Clients may be socialized into therapy through a language system that emphasizes pejorative labels and suggests that therapists hold specialized knowledge that, in truth, they may or may not possess. Therapists may give clients the implicit or explicit message that something is wrong or flawed with them, which, in turn, may contribute to negative treatment effects. (p. 247)

In therapy and in our publications for public consumption, social scientists and mental health professionals have an enormous power in that the stories they offer people to understand their lives become their personal stories and experience. More importantly, they have it in their power to either normalize or pathologize events: that is, to provide either stories that can offer hope or those that lead to despair. Thus, as Schofield (1986) observed, as a function of the criteria by which we make a diagnosis, we can influence the proportion of the population that is defined as either mentally healthy or mentally ill. Schofield's observation seems consistent with the suggestion that the concepts of mental illness and family dysfunction are invented realities. Thus, the incidence of mental illness and family dysfunction is relative to the rigor of the standards developed by professionals.

While social scientists and mental health professionals play an important part in alleviating pain and suffering, they also participate in creating the stories that people use to experience themselves and their relationships. Typically, they work within the ideology of the society. In other words, traditional mental health practice is a licensed and officially sanctioned role. Such official recognition is only given if they agree to practice in ways that are logically consistent with the ideology of the society. Professional organizations, accrediting bodies, and licensing boards serve gate-keeping functions. Quality of preparation for practice is an important issue, but ideological and political correctness is equally important.

The stories through which we live our lives can be self-defeating, in that the attempted solutions they describe not only may not solve the problem but also may make the problem worse (Keeney, 1983; Wátzlawick et al., 1974). Minuchin (1984) asserted, "Answers are born in the way we pose questions" (p. 45). Or as Alan Watts (1972) noted, "Problems that remain persistently insoluble should always be suspected as questions asked in the wrong way" (p. 54). In our work with our clients, we listen to the stories in which our clients live their lives or, as we prefer to say, live their lives for them; we help them ask different questions that may offer solutions where the solutions offered by the original questions only exacerbate the problem. However, we can ask different questions only if we begin to tell ourselves a different story about the circumstance that we are experiencing as problematic. And this we cannot do unless we have an awareness that the experience of a particular problem in need of solution is only possible from a story that defines that experience as problematic.

Given such an awareness, the following chapters may be seen as exercises in story repair or story reconstruction. In effect, we give people permission to create, select, and begin to live their lives in an alternate story. It is important to note that no alternative story is "true"; however, it may be more useful for certain purposes. It is our belief that it is even more useful if any alternative story is viewed as a story. We believe that an awareness that our human experience is socially constructed opens the door to more possibilities as we are empowered to construct our own realities. If people live their lives in this way, then living will not necessarily be easier. One would need to live with a measure of uncertainty. Indeed, some might find such a life intolerable and seek gurus, the experts, and the professionals who are more than willing to write scripts for people's lives.

The following conversation between Gregory Bateson and Stewart Brand (Brand, 1974) seems to be an appropriate way to close this chapter:

"You cannot induce a Pavlovian nervous breakdown—what do they call it, 'experimental neurosis'—in an animal out in the field."

"I didn't know that!"

More of the Bateson chortle. "You've got to have a lab."

"Why?"

"Because the smell of the lab, the feel of the harness in which the animal stands and all that are context markers which say what sort of thing is going on in this situation; that you're supposed to be right or wrong, for example."

"What you do is to induce these neuroses is, you train the animal to believe that the smell of the lab and similar things is a message which tells him he's got to discriminate between an ellipse and a circle, say. Right. He learns to discriminate. Then you make the discrimination a little more difficult, and he learns again, and you have underlined the message. Then you make the discrimination impossible.

"At this point discrimination is not the appropriate form of behavior. Guesswork is. But the animal cannot stop feeling that he ought to discriminate, and then you get the symptomatology coming on. The one whose discrimination broke down was the experimenter, who failed to discriminate between the context for discrimination and a context for gambling."

"So," says I, "it's the experimenter's neurosis that . . . has now become the experimental neurosis of the animal. The whole context has a Heisenberg hook in it much worse than the atoms ever thought of." (Atomic physicist Heisenberg's famous uncertainty principle states that the observer constantly alters what he observes by the meddling act of observation.)

"In the field what happens?"

"None of this happens. For one thing, the stimuli don't count. Those electric shocks they use are about as powerful as what the animal would get if he pricked his leg on a bramble, pushing through."

"Suppose you've got an animal whose job in life is to turn over stones and eat the beetles under them. All right, one stone in ten is going to have a beetle under it. He cannot go into a nervous breakdown because the nine stones don't have beetles under them. But the lab can make him do that, you see."

"Do you think we're all in a lab of our own making, in which we drive each other crazy?"

"You said it, not I, brother," chuckling. "Of course." (pp. 25–27)

Chapter 5

On the Clinical Bias

One of the advantages or curses of the human species is our ability to reflect upon ourselves or to think about our thinking. This chapter provides you with an experience about the stories you use to think about yourself, your relationships, your family, and your society. Social science and mental health professionals have an important role in creating theories that people use in reflecting upon themselves. The invention of a professional theory (story) about people, relationships, families, and society is but a short step away from becoming a story that people use to think about themselves, their lives, their relationships, and their society. Thus, professional discourse becomes a part of social discourse. In Western ideology, the model that characterizes socially acceptable ways of thinking is called the "deficit model." The deficit model implies a sickness or inadequacy bias—a "disorder."

In brief, an assumption of the deficit model is that all people growing up in a seriously troubled home will become seriously damaged adults. A variation of the deficit model is that whatever your accomplishments or virtues, there is always another aspect of yourself in which you are deficient. Most theories of psychotherapy, counseling, and family therapy created by clinicians and social science researchers involve the deficit model. Bateson (in Brand, 1974) referred to this as the "clinical bias." He wrote,

On the damage that's been done to psychiatric thinking by the clinical bias. The clinical bias being, that there are good things and there are bad things. The bad things necessarily have causes. This is not so true of good things. (p. 25)

In merging the designs for lives ("supposed to be's and do's" and "not supposed to be's and do's") implicit in these same theories with the clinical bias, one is oriented to focus on the "bad things" and the search for and elimination of the "bad things" from one's life, relationships, and family. This bias lives in most medical-model theories of psychotherapy. The assumption is that you must get at the underlying "causes" of these bad things, and once you get to the underlying causes, you will no longer have the problem. The search for "causes" of the "bad things" is implicit in the why question that is a part of the commonsense psychology in our culture. If there is a bad thing, then there must be a cause. And more often than not, believing in the concept of linear time, we search for the cause in the past, and one can be created by establishing a connection between a childhood trauma or experience with an alcoholic parent or dysfunctional family. The fixation on the bad things or the way I am that I am not "supposed to be and do" reflects a design for the way people, relationships, and families are "supposed to be and do" "Bad things necessarily have causes."

Bad things have an etiology and reflect cultural biases and values. In a class one of us was teaching, a gay man was making a presentation on the gay experience. In a question-and-answer period after the presentation, a student asked, "What is the etiology of homosexuality?" The presenter responded to the question with the standard biological and sociological answers that research reflecting the clinical bias provides. The instructor, alert to what he calls "teaching moments," presented the following idea, which some students found disconcerting "I suggest you ask also about the etiology of heterosexuality." But then, such a question is not consistent with the clinical bias. Only bad things and things not valued by the society necessarily have causes.

"This is not so true of good things." In most people's lives there are at least as many good things that happen as bad things, even in the most stringent designs for how people are supposed to be. But then, some people do not allow these good things to impinge on their consciousness. Gadamer (1996) wrote,

> We are not permanently aware of health, we do not anxiously carry it with us as we do an illness. It is not something that invites or demands permanent attention. Rather it belongs to that miraculous capacity we have to forget ourselves. (p. 96)

An important social control mechanism in all societies that carries over into therapeutic practice is to create a conscious awareness in ourselves and others of deviations or differences and the guilt one feels when one or others have not lived up to the standard. The clinical bias focuses our attention away from these good things, which are often taken for granted and are without cause or dismissed, with a "Yes, but . . ." The clinical bias has become a powerful and painful part of our experience in our normative medical-model therapies. This is especially true when prescribed ways of being are utopian.

The number of bad things that happen in one's life for which one must search for causes includes just about every imbalance on every normative

standard set forth by normative social scientists and mental health professionals. Thus, one is doomed to a lifetime search for the causes of the bad
things. Of course, one big cause can be defined as the source of many of the
imbalances on the dimensions set forth by normative social science. Several
big causes are popular in today's social science and mental health market.
One of the most popular is being an "adult child of a dysfunctional family"
or a childhood experience that is viewed as traumatic. A cartoon text came to
mind as we wrote this:

THERAPIST: "Were you abused as a child?"

CLIENT: "If you say so."

This provides a rich source of "cause" for many of the problems and "bad"
things you may experience in your life (which you may not have experienced
if you didn't know they were bad things). The flip side of the coin, of course,
is that if you are identified as being an adult child of a dysfunctional family,
then you must, by definition, have problems and bad things happening in
your life of which you may be unaware. Some therapists are quite good at
alerting clients to problems of which they were unaware. Further, in today's
social science and mental health market, the concept of a dysfunctional family includes almost any family that does not have the perfect configuration
and processes as defined by normative social science and mental health. As
we surmised in Chapter 3, it may take many years of therapy to overcome the
effects of an idyllic childhood so that one may become normal like the rest
of us. If you view your childhood as idyllic and have problems in living, then
obviously you have overlooked some things—repressed memories revisited.

But in every life, in every relationship and family, good things do happen. And if we transcend the clinical bias and allow ourselves to experience
the good things or to search in therapy and in life for the causes of the good
things with the same passion that we search for the causes of the bad things,
then many mental health professionals would be unnecessary. How do people
celebrate themselves, and how do family members celebrate each other?
And, while it may sound strange, it is possible that the good things and bad
things that one experiences may have the same "cause." It is inconsistent with
commonsense psychology and counter to most theories of therapy to assert
that the same childhood trauma or experience with an alcoholic parent or a
life-threatening traumatic event may also be the "cause" of the good things
that happen in one's life. Answers are born in the questions asked. Resilience
may be one outcome. Opportunity may be another. Consider Watts's story of
the Chinese farmer:

There was a Chinese farmer whose horse ran away.
All the neighbors gathered in the evening and said, "That's too bad."
The farmer said, "Maybe."

The next day the horse came back and brought with it seven wild horses.
The neighbors said, "Aren't you lucky."
The farmer said, "Maybe."

The next day the farmer's son tried to break in one of the wild horses and broke his leg.
And the neighbors said, "That's too bad."
The farmer said, "Maybe."

The next day the conscription officers came for men for the army, and the son was rejected.
The neighbors said, "Isn't that great? Your son got out of serving in the army."
The farmer said, "Maybe." (in Mindfulness 360, 2017)

The moral of this tale is that in our limited human perspective, we cannot always see in which direction progress lies.

Chapter 6

Conceptual Bites in Summary
of the Paradox

There seems to be an increase in messages that would soothe, inspire, engender hope, and more. Useful, perhaps, but they also cannot not make us consciously aware of the degree to which we experience or live our lives in accordance with the message. However well intentioned, they provide standards by which we judge ourselves and others.

There may be a limit to living our lives self-consciously—of which we become aware in our higher-order self-consciousness. Oyle and Jean (1992) wrote, "Have you noticed that one part of you does things and another part of you watches?" (p. 17). There is another part of "you" that watches the first-level watcher. The concept of "enough" comes to mind. How much of anything—material or conceptual—is enough? What are the consequences of watching ourselves and others too closely?

Any increase in self-consciousness, especially self-consciousness about our self-consciousness, can lead to enlightenment, or it can feed the experience of craziness. They may be the same. We suspect that artists in all mediums— sculpture, drawing, painting, music, poetry, and so on—may experience the craziness that enlightenment may provide. Maybe all people need the same latitude that our societies allow artists. Remember also that en*light*enment is conceptually connected to darkening.

Therapy has lost its taboo status. It has become more socially acceptable. Indeed, not being in therapy may be a sign that you need to be in therapy. Being in therapy may have become a sign of mental health. It may be a litmus test for people in relationships. Therapy can be therapeutic or toxic. It can help us solve some persistent problems. However, the solutions to persistent problems cannot not create other problems—sometimes less serious and sometimes more serious. Responsible (and ethical?) therapists will encourage exploration of the consequences of any solution with their clients. Also, these therapists will encourage exploration of how the solution will affect other people in their social network.

We monitor ourselves and others for signs of deviation from standard, accepted, prescribed protocols in behavior and experience. We may interpret these deviations as signs of mental illness—a concept that is integral to interpreting our experience of self and others. We compare ourselves and others to standards that at a higher level are rightly viewed as arbitrary but at another level of life are prescriptive and expected.

Mental illness and mental health are concepts that are part of our language systems and professional and popular discourse. How would we language and conceptualize our experience and behavior and experiences of others without these concepts? There are other options.

Substance abuse might be usefully viewed as cutting down "monkey chatter"—coping with paradoxes and contradictions implicit in worldviews of societies. It may also be a means of transcending the concepts for living and experiencing the whole that is lost when we make distinctions—create parts of a whole that is our world. Mindfulness, Zen, and Buddhist meditation practices may seek the same relief—respite from our crazy-making worldviews.

Other options may be opened to us if our self- and other assessments and assessments of professionals included viewing people in the different contexts in which they live. People are somewhat different in different contexts: crazy in some, not so crazy in others.

Illness is easier to discuss than health (G. Bateson, 1972). As in a game, it is easier to describe the rules of a game by what is not allowed than it is what is allowed. Descriptions of illness are articulate and extensive. One may be at a loss for words when asked to describe feeling well. Gadamer (1996) describes, we are not permanently aware of health, we do not anxiously carry it with us as we do an illness. It is not something that invites or demands permanent attention. Rather it belongs to that miraculous capacity we have to forget ourselves. (p. 96)

"Health does not actually present itself to us. Of course, one can also attempt to establish standard values for health. But the attempt to impose these standard values on a healthy individual would only result in making the person ill. It lies in the nature of health that it sustains its own proper balance and proportion. The appeal to standard values which are derived by averaging out different empirical data and then simply applied to particular cases is inappropriate to determining health and cannot be forced upon it" (Gadamer, 1996, p. 107).

Any standard value involves comparison to what is not valued. People are error activated. We notice deviations from the standard value and, as with health, not compliance. We notice difference or deviation that activates efforts to bring people into compliance. Thus, therapists are invited to the party.

The problems of all clients in therapy involve deviation from standards that reflect values. The theories of therapists involve diagnostics that reflect the standards and values of the society in which they work and sanctions their roles. Indeed, the attempt to impose standard values on a healthy individual (couple, family, or other system) would only result in making the person (couple, family, or other system) ill.

Therapy seeks to be and purports to be therapeutic, but it may be toxic. Its toxicity may be fed by the concept of mental illness—a broad-sweep term that includes deviations from standards. The diagnosis that one is mentally ill explains everything and nothing.

Standards are necessary in any society. They choreograph the dance between people in the society and the institutions of the society.

Diagnostic categories are social constructions that reflect standards and values. They are arbitrary in that they reflect the values of the culture that constructs the categories for diagnostics. Different culture = different values, different standards, and different diagnostic categories.

Standardization of problems requires standardization of "treatments," which requires standardization of clients. It is a perfect storm—a closed system that rarely questions itself. Differences in "treatment" are variations within the same paradigm.

Attempts to prevent mental illness by calling attention to it cannot not increase self-consciousness and exploration about whether one has that which attempts are designed to describe and prevent. Indeed, attempts to promote mental health and prevent mental illness increases self-consciousness about standards. Recall Gadamer (1996): "But the attempt to impose these standard values on a healthy individual would only result in making the person ill" (p. 107).

People may be diagnosed as mentally ill by standards, but that may not be their experience.

Are people who experience themselves as mentally ill, mentally ill or "sane"?

People who view themselves as sane may be diagnosed as mentally ill.

In a context for the purpose of diagnosis, how would one demonstrate that one is not mentally ill or is mentally ill?

The process of taking any psychological inventory cannot not feed our self-consciousness—even intelligence tests. In taking an intelligence test or inventory, we cannot not self-consciously wonder about our own level of intelligence or deviance as we compare ourselves to the value or standard implicit in each item and the whole inventory. We are also self-consciously aware of the context that is the purpose for the administration of the instrument. Who will view the results and what values guide their viewing—and hence their judgment?

Indeed, the person who takes the inventory may be different for having taken the inventory—so that the "validity" of the results should be suspect. Of course, this assumes that one can observe without affecting the person being observed.

Maybe therapy should be a philosophical experience. The therapist would help clients evolve an epistemology that has a conscious awareness of itself. A beginning might be asking, "What do you value?" rather than "What is the problem for which you seek therapy?" or "What standard are you using to compare your experience that suggests you have a problem?" A therapist might also ask, "How is that a problem for you?" or "What do you anticipate would be better?" or, "Is this a problem that you believe you have or a problem that others believe you have?" or, "What problems would you prefer instead of your current problems?" The problems they present and their visions of getting better reveal their values as well as concepts and expectations from their worldviews.

"Please stop trying to help me! Your suggestions and attempted solutions are creating higher-order and more serious problems. After due deliberation and with your help, I prefer to keep the problems I now have. The standards of expected performance are more freeing."

What are the limits of benevolence? When do our actions of doing good become harmful?

"In essence, there is a problem of a reverse approach to diagnosis; we may define as mentally ill any person who does not have perfect mental health, and we may define perfect mental health in terms of such rigorous standards that it is a condition notable for its absence rather than its presence in a majority of the population at a given time" (Schofield, 1986, p. 12).

"What has changed is man's relative freedom to think about his condition, to be anxious about his anxiety, and to live in a cultural epoch which entertains the thesis that personal frustration of any sort is abnormal, that avoidance of anxiety should be a primary personal goal and that society can provide the experts for the successful prevention of unhappiness" (Schofield, 1986, p. 44).

Schofield (1986) suggested that as more and more mental health practitioners join the ranks, there is an increasing need for more clients who "need" the services provided by the professionals. Thus, as more professionals rely for their livelihood on clientele in need of their services, more and more clients "appear" or, as Schofield suggested, are "invented" by narrowing the range of what constitutes "normalcy."

There seems to be an economic and political aspect to diagnosis: "Those persons who pay the highest fees for psychotherapy will tend to have the mildest degrees of maladjustments" (Schofield, 1986, p. 19).

"It is not commonly recognized that, for a given culture, the extent and nature of mental illness is a function of relativistic definition which is variable over time—being one time rigorous, conservative, and applicable to small numbers of persons, being another time loose, liberal and appropriate to huge numbers. . . . The greater the number of psychiatrists, psychologists, and other trained mental health experts in the population, the greater the higher the incidence of mental illness" (Schofield, 1986, p. 13).

I have an eating disorder, a drinking disorder, a smoking disorder, an intimacy disorder. I joined a support group for my disorders. I go to my groups seven nights and three afternoons a week. I couldn't live without them. I have a support group disorder. (Author unknown)

"Second-order cybernetics and the work of Maturana (Maturana & Varela, 1992) have influenced our ideas about effecting change. With regard to interventions, we believe it is unwise to attempt to ascertain what is 'really' going on with a particular family or what the 'real' problem is. Recognizing what is 'real,' whether it be the problem or the intervention, is always a consequence of our social construction (Keeney, 1992). Keeney further states that since family clinicians join their clients in the social construction of a therapeutic reality, the clinician is also responsible 'for the universe of experience that is created' (1982, p. 165). Maturana (1988) presents another twist on this critical notion of reality by submitting that individuals (living systems) draw forth reality—they do not construct it, nor does it exist independent of them" (Wright & Leahy, 1994, p. 382).

"We are inevitably prisoners of time, place and culture. The significance of history lies far less in the facts unearthed or the events described than in the determination of the [W]eltanschauung, about which people are largely unaware but without which the facts and events cannot be comprehended. A weltanschauung is not motivated, it is received, imbibed, a kind of given, a basic outline within which motivation gets direction" (Sarason, 1981, p. 47).

The scripts of the cultural stories we are supposed to live by are too narrow to be livable. How should life be? How should relationships be? What is possible? There will always be challenges. There must be room for error and anomalies. There will always be problems in living and negotiating relationships. Life is just one damned thing after another—interspersed with experiences of joy. But the more we focus on deviance from unrealistic standards, the experiences of joy may become less frequent. It is through these challenges and surviving the damned things that happen that we build up resilience.

Chapter 7

Wondering

Philosopher Arne Næss (with Haukeland, 2002) wrote, "For Philosophy begins and ends with wondering—profound wondering" (p. 3). He also wrote, "By and large it is painful to think" (p. 13). In the chapters you have just read, we sought to have you become philosophers and wonderers as well as to think—particularly to think about your thinking about therapy. So if you are wondering and thinking (or even objecting), then we have been successful.

In the introduction to this book, we wondered about several things. Primarily we wondered about whether the normative, medical model was an appropriate paradigm to meet the challenge of what we believe is a pandemic of mental illness. We also wondered about the possibility that normative, medical-model attempts to "treat" the pandemic may be contributing to an increase in the incidence of and severity of mental illness. Thus, we suggest that the attempted solutions to the problem of the pandemic may have become the problem (Wátzlawick et al., 1974).

That remains the primary issue we wonder about. There are many other things we wonder about related to that issue. We share a few of them in this chapter:

- We don't wonder about the pain, frustration, anxiety, fear, confusion, sadness, and more that people experience as they try to find meaning or purpose or just survive everyday problems while living in today's world. The world is ever changing at an accelerating pace, with spiritual, economic, relationship, political, and ecological challenges adding to personal challenges.
- We wonder about the concept of mental illness. *Mental* locates the problem in the individual, with no or little regard for the ideology or social context

from which the "mental illness" evolves. The individual's pain is increased when their logical attempted solutions to problems are not working. Should problems in living and problems in making transitions in life be described as mental illnesses? But of course, the concept of mental illness that locates the problem in individuals relieves societies of doing therapy on the crazy-making rules for living contained within its Weltanschauungs.

- We don't wonder that some "disorders" like schizophrenia, ADHD, and autism may have a genetic or biological base. We wonder about how inter-personal contexts and assigning a diagnostic metaphor to the symptoms may serve to maintain the difference. People so diagnosed (indeed all people) are interactive (Hacking, 1999) and are consciously aware of the diagnostic categories and stories used to describe their experiences. People are conscious of seeing and being seen—or perceiving and being perceived. Indeed, other people in their interpersonal networks who are aware of the diagnosis may maintain or exacerbate the problem. We don't relate to people; we relate to the stories we tell ourselves about people. Biology is just one part of the story.

- Like Thomas Szasz (1970), we wonder about punctuating mental illness as a disease, a designation that locates it in the field of medicine and acti-vates the terms *treatment* and *psychopharmacology*. In a totally connected universe, the body cannot not be affected by the incredible challenges experienced while attempting to live in a society. But a focus on the brain chemistry as the sole cause and the primary focus for treatment ignores ideological, psychological, and interpersonal dimensions to that which is called mental illness.

- We don't wonder about the search for causes of mental illness because the concept of cause is consistent with the normative, medical-disease model. However, while the concept of cause may include context, the primary focus for "treatment" remains the individual. Indeed, inquiry about the contexts in which "mental illness" occurs may be more useful than search-ing for the cause.

- We wonder if looking at context would be more fruitful than a search for cause. The concept of context is consistent with the systems perspective, which would see mental illness not as an anomaly but as a logical response and role that complements other roles and concepts in a society. Viewing mental illness in context would normalize rather than view it as a pathol-ogy. Again, how "mental illness" evolves in context may be a more useful question than a search for cause when context is the focus of inquiry.

- We wonder about "treatments" focusing on parts: either mind, body, or social context—psycho, bio, socio—ignoring the necessary connection between them. Any perturbation of one cannot not affect the others.

- We wonder about fitting people into categories or constructs—the standardization of "disorders" that evolve standardized treatments and standardized clients. Indeed, while this is how we "know" and converse, standardization misses uniqueness.
- We wonder about how the designation of a Mental Health Awareness Month, awareness days for specific disorders, and checklists and warning signs of "mental illness" contribute to increasing sensitivity to normal problems in living and to having people wonder about being mentally ill. Mental health awareness cannot not also be mental illness awareness.
- We wonder about the process of Googling symptoms when people feel distress of any kind and selecting those that fit a disorder and ignoring those that do not. This process may convince them that they have a disorder.
- We wonder about what Hacking (1995) calls the "looping effect." The process of diagnosis, while intended to be purely descriptive, cannot not have the effect of describing how people should feel and behave. Normative, medical-model diagnostic processes assume that one can observe without affecting. While this may be "true" when observing a stone or a quark, humans are "interactive"—aware of being observed (Hacking, 1999). Any description of "what is" also describes "what it is not."
- We wonder about how a diagnosis of mental illness may serve to absolve one of responsibility, a feeling that is reinforced by medicalizing the problem. When viewed from a systemic (interactional) perspective, being absolved of responsibility can be both useful and an impediment relative to context.
- We wonder about how what clearly is a relationship problem with a couple necessitates the diagnosis of a disorder if they are to be reimbursed by insurance. The issue then becomes which of the two will accept the diagnosis.
- We wonder about how organizations (corporations) that are invested in treating mental illnesses also have an investment in maintaining or increasing the incidence of mental illnesses.
- We don't wonder how American (and most Western) ideologies have an investment in supporting the concept of mental illness. Thus, supporting the view that mental illness is a problem of the individual, the contradictory and paradoxical (crazy-making) elements in a society's worldview need not be seriously challenged. Indeed, most therapies focus on promoting adjustment to prevailing norms for living rather than challenging these norms.
- We wonder about how "evidence-based" treatments for specific disorders limit therapeutic options to fit the uniqueness of each person. Again, standardized diagnoses require standardized treatments for standardized clients. One size does not fit all.
- We wonder about how a construct for a disorder may become a primary identity for a client—in some cases, when no "treatment" is successful and

even when it relieves symptoms, it is a life sentence. People are interactive and aware of the stories being told about them, which they may assume and maintain as a primary identity.

- We wonder about how people in a client's social network relate to and maintain the disorder. We don't relate to people; we relate to the stories (metaphors) we tell ourselves about people. Thus, the behavior of people in a client's social network complements and maintains the symptomatic behavior and identity. The process is reciprocal in that both parties in a relationship are aware of the stories each tells the other—an awareness that maintains the status quo of the relationship.
- We wonder if the symptoms of a "mental illness" may be adaptive to survive in a crazy-making context of social relationships. Jay Haley (1976) suggested that "symptoms are tactics" in control of relationships or survival in relationships that are double-binding. Keeney (1983) suggests that every problem is a solution to another problem.
- We wonder whether the increase in inspiring messages that seek to soothe, inspire, engender hope, and so on may be both useful *and* detrimental. Any such message may activate a self-conscious awareness of how one measures up to the ideal set forth.
- We wonder about the consequences of therapy as being more socially acceptable. Is not being in therapy a sign that you need to be in therapy? Has being in therapy become a sign of mental health? Has being in therapy become a litmus test for relationships? Has not being in therapy become a litmus test to wonder about what problems one is denying?
- We wonder about how universities respond to the increased incidence of mental illness by educating more therapists in the medical model to deal with the pandemic. Reports of waiting lists for therapy confirm this need. Does the supply of therapists create its own demand? Viewed systemically, the concepts of supply and demand are reciprocal—recursive (Schofield, 1986).
- We wonder about the concept of mental health. Is mental health the absence of symptomatic behavior or experience? Can *mental health* be defined in ways that do not involve absence of symptoms? Can asking the question, "Are you mentally healthy?" not activate questions about "mental illness"?
- We wonder, consistent with William Schofield (1986), whether therapists have the knowledge and skill to successfully prevent unhappiness?
- We wonder whether the criteria for mental health may be so utopian that it is notable for its absence rather than its presence in our societies? What role does an attitude that "life happens" play in the degree to which people experience themselves and others as mentally ill?
- And now a very big wonder: Unlike inanimate objects, people are interactive (Hacking, 1999). That is, they are consciously aware of being observed.

They are consciously aware of the words and categories used to describe them. They are aware of the stories told about the categories and words that include them. And, as mentioned earlier, people who observe others relate to the words or categories or stories they tell themselves about a person. This is a reciprocal process. The important point here is this awareness of the stories being told about the category or word may lead one to internalize, experience, and behave in a manner logically consistent with the category or word.

As an example, currently there is much alarm and concern about adolescents (adolescence). Popular news publishes professional descriptions of adolescents that include the challenges and transitions of "being adolescents." These stories that purport to describe the internal turmoil of these interactive beings may in fact create their internal turmoil. Moreover, when children enter adolescence, they, too, are aware of the inner turmoil described by professionals and relate with heightened alertness to symptoms of the inner turmoil. Self-fulfilling prophecies? This is not to imply that the inner turmoil experienced by some adolescents is not real, but it is a big wonder to believe that it evolves within the adolescent and peers, independent of observers. Adolescents are watching, listening, and experiencing the stories being told about them, and they experience the different ways parents and adults relate to them. Thus, we wonder whether the attempted solutions to solve the problem of adolescents' inner turmoil and potential suicidal ideation may participate in bringing forth that reality. From the perspective of second-order cybernetics—that is, participant and observer—this effect is inevitable. One cannot just observe. Observation in therapy, through psychological instruments, checklists, warning signs, and any activity that promotes self-conscious comparisons and assessing, is participation, and the observer constructs the reality of the persons being observed. There are no independent variables when adolescents seek their grounding by observing other adolescents.

Rusty Berkus (1990) described the process as follows: "For it is the look on the face of the Other that gives us our sense of self" (p. 27). And the look on our faces reflects the stories we tell about another person. What look is on your face with another who has been diagnosed with bipolar or borderline personality disorder? What is the look on the face of the other when they seek grounding when the face of the other is also seeking grounding? What look on the face of the other would promote the experience of being appreciated, accepted, and "normal" even when the person being observed is distressed or challenged?

Coming full circle, one recent survey found that 90 percent of Americans were concerned about mental illness. We wonder about the effects of hue and cry and hypochondria about mental illness. Indeed, even the customary greeting, "How are you doing?" may take a more serious meaning. We wonder about how much more serious and more frequent the problem may be when politicians, economists, and entrepreneurs intervene. We wonder about the difference it would make if the therapy experience were normalizing rather than pathologizing or being on alert for symptoms of disorders.

- We wonder about what Bateson (in Brand, 1974) referred to as the clinical bias, that being there are good things and bad things. The bad things necessarily have causes. This is not so true of good things. Thus, we are alert for deviations and seek causes for them. Good things just happen.
- We don't wonder about the efficacy of placebos. Indeed, sugar pills have been demonstrated to be as effective as medications under some circumstances, and the attitude of the physician who prescribes the medication can augment the effectiveness of the medication. Indeed, placebos can be effective even if the patient is aware they are taking a placebo (Kaptchuk, 2023). The placebo effect in therapy might be the therapist's confidence that the therapy experience will be effective.
- But then we wonder about the nocebo effect—"being informed of a pill or procedure's potential side effects is enough to bring about real life-like symptoms" (Stromberg, 2012). In his study, when patients were told that they might experience some pain as a result of a medical procedure, they experienced more pain than those who were not told. The context of therapy and diagnostic questions asked are not value neutral and may activate self-conscious wondering about mental health and illness. Of course, a retort might be "We are merely uncovering (discovering) what is already there." This is consistent with the assumption that one can observe without affecting—normative, medical-model practice. We simply suggest that in therapy and in our models of prevention, there may be a nocebo effect—consistent with higher-order cybernetics.

It seems that we are the only species that wonders—or at least that is a story we tell ourselves. Animals in the wild go about their business not worrying about their relationships, even with other species, and do not wonder about their purpose in and meaning for their lives. Indeed, while some species feel love, grief, care, and concern (to attribute human terms to them), they do not have psychological or relationship problems. It does seem that they may develop psychological problems when we "domesticate" them. Montaigne (in Bakewell, 2010) wrote about animals, "We find it hard to understand them, he says, but they must find it just as hard to understand us. This defect that hinders communication between us, why is it not just as much ours as theirs?" (p. 137). Montaigne cannot look at his cat without seeing her looking back at him and imagining himself as he looks at her (p. 138). Indeed, we may look at each other and wonder about our own craziness and that of others. If we believe in it, then we will see it. The theory decides what we will see.

We have shared some of our wonderings in this and previous chapters. We hope to plant the seeds for you to develop an epistemology that has a conscious awareness of itself. We hope to replace certainty with uncertainty and wondering. And in your uncertainty, you might find utility in systems theory and social constructionism—and find some pragmatics in its philosophy. We share our story with the hope that it may tweak the hardened categories of normative, medical-model therapeutic practice. In effect we seek to help you become philosophers more consciously. Indeed, the alternative model based on systems theory and social constructionism would help clients become philosophers, as well. Helping clients develop an epistemology that has a conscious awareness of itself may serve them better than "treating disorders" or "solving problems." But therapists cannot facilitate a therapeutic process to this end unless they have become wonderers.

In Part II, we explicate systems theory and social constructionism as alternative approaches to therapy that may be useful antidotes to the normative, medical model for therapy, which we believe may be contributing to rather than curtailing the pandemic of mental illness.

Part II

SYSTEMIC AND SOCIAL CONSTRUCTIONIST CONCEPTS AND PROCESSES FOR THERAPY

Chapter 8

About Systems Theory, Constructivism, and Social Constructionism

In this chapter, we present our story of systems theory, constructivism, and social constructionism. We contrast systems theory and therapy with what we refer to as normative, medical-model mental health and therapy theory and practice in which the individual is the primary unit of analysis. As you may recall, from the systems perspective, relationships are the primary units of analysis, not the individual. From normative, medical models of theory and practice, systems theory and family therapy are often viewed as an alternative treatment modality for "mental illness" rather than as a different paradigm, which challenges the medical model in fundamental ways. From the systemic paradigm, symptomatic behavior construed as mental illness is not viewed as an anomaly but rather as a logical product of the interactional and conceptual dynamics of social systems. The systems paradigm challenges the very foundation of traditional mental health practice in fundamental ways—particularly at the level of higher-order cybernetics. Therapeutic theory and practice from the normative, medical model fits Western ideologies into which people in general and professional therapists in particular, are socialized.

This includes the following characteristics:

- a priority above all else to autonomy and individual responsibility;
- a belief that there is not anything we cannot overcome if we work at it hard enough;
- faith in the ability of science to provide solutions to problems;
- commitment to a work ethic according to which economic success is equated with virtue and failure is seen as a moral weakness; and
- the assumption that there is a reality out there that we can know, predict, and control.

So with this introduction, we tell our story.

Normative mental health practice based on the medical model follows a sequence somewhat like the following: assessment, diagnosis, treatment planning, and implementation of the treatment plan until the solution of the problem. Assessment is not a tabula rasa or blank-slate process. It is value laden. Assessment necessarily involves making (or using existing socially approved) distinctions and comparing people relative to some standard. Although it may vary in specific content, it involves assessment relative to some "supposed to be" or "not supposed to be" and a comparison of how much or how little of the "supposed to be" or "not supposed to be" the client system has relative to some norm group against which the client's performance is compared. Thus, all assessment is relative to some theory, which reflects values, which reflects the norms of the society, of which the therapist is a part. In effect, we don't assess problems; we assess values and the degree to which a person, couple, or family lives up to the values of their society or culture. Without values, no behavior or experience can be defined or experienced as problematic or acceptable. These values are lived in the collective consciousness and language of the societies. They are social constructions. Systems theory would have us view problems (disorders) as evolving in relationships and as maintained in relationships.

The practice of research necessarily involves observation as we attempt to know and discover facts. Observation in normative mental health practice suggests that the process of assessment is an objective, nonintrusive process; that is, it assumes that one *can stand outside of, observe* directly or indirectly using some inventory or instrument, and *discover* what is really going on in the client. Thus, seeing is believing. This view is consistent with simple cybernetics or first-order systems theory. First-order systems theory assumes that everybody and everything in the universe is connected. However, in making this assertion or observation, it assumes that the observer is outside the system being observed—thus is "objective." Thus, the first-order cybernetics perspective is inconsistent with its assertion of a totally interconnected universe. It excludes the observer who asserts that all is connected except the observer. The family-therapy models of Bowen, Minuchin, Satir, Nagy, and Whitaker and therapies based on personality theories, while useful, are first-order cybernetics models. That is, each diagnosed dysfunction in family systems has a prescription for successful family and personal functioning. Therapists from these models punctuate themselves as independent observers outside the system. Again, all first-order therapy models may be quite useful, and processes from these models can be used in therapy, but they are inconsistent with the systemic concept of a totally interconnected universe.

Second-order systems or cybernetics theory is consistent with the concept of a totally interconnected universe and suggests that the very process of observing is participating in influencing the nature of what one is observing (quantum physics—the Heisenberg principle). It also suggests that because one cannot not be a part of the assessment relationship, one does not discover; rather, one invents or creates (constructs) the reality that becomes the lens through which clients will begin to see themselves. Believing is seeing. Thus, any client being observed may be—and perhaps cannot not be—self-conscious of the fact of being observed. They are interactive (Hacking, 1999). If one uses the California Personality Inventory rather than the Minnesota Multiphasic Personality Inventory as an observation tool, a very different profile will result, and the items as well as the story of the profile as filtered through the lens of the therapist will influence the reality experienced by the client. Neither is an "objective" measure of a real reality that exists within the client. Each is a value-laden measure that provides clients with a value-laden experience of themselves. Effectively the instrument becomes a prosthesis of the theory or value frame of the therapist. The questions asked or not asked by the therapist also comprise an instrument.

From the perspective of higher-order or second-order cybernetics or systems theory, observation is intervention, or because the observer is part of the unit being observed, a better word is *perturbation*, which implies a view from within rather than a view from outside the client system. Thus, a description of a client (or any person or phenomenon) may say more about the describer than the person being described. In effect, the concept of environment as that which is outside of or separate from an entity self-destructs and is replaced by the concept of context that includes the observer—that to which you necessarily belong has no outside for you.

In effect the "science of discovering a real reality" self-destructs when the process is viewed through the lens of cybernetics of cybernetics, social constructionism, and constructivism. The process of social science research is viewed as value based. Any "facts" discovered by a social scientist are framework specific and relative as well as reflecting the values of the society of which the social scientist and its instrument is a part. The appropriate words for the outcome of scientific investigation are *invention* and *construction* rather than *discovery*.

Science based on Newtonian mechanics is discovery oriented. It suggests that what is observed is a mirror image of what is "out there" (objective). Science based on quantum mechanics is invention oriented (construction). We cannot know what is really "out there." What we can see "out there" is relative to what we believe is out there. Thus, believing is seeing rather than seeing is believing. Moreover, and perhaps more importantly, what you observe out there cannot not be affected by the very act of observing it. From the systems paradigm and quantum physics, when we look at the world, we are looking at ourselves looking in a mirror (Briggs & Peat, 1984).

In effect there is no "real reality" "out there" that we can know with certainty. The very process of attempting to discover what is really out there creates the reality that we believe exists out there. (Interestingly, the concept of perception implies that there is a reality out there, but we cannot know what it is with any certainty.) Of course, to be consistent with the perspective we are offering, in asserting that the "real reality" we cannot know, we are constructing an alternative "real reality." Thus, our assertion must include itself in the proposition that it is asserting. This is the paradox, the problem of self-reference with which we must live. We offer a higher-order paradigm, but it contradicts itself by its own logic. However, this higher-order view opens the door for different "real realities," each of which has very different consequences for life, living, and therapy. Perspectives need not be true or describe what is really going on to be useful in therapy or in life. This is not to deny that things (the Holocaust, genocide, slavery) do not happen. Please note that even naming the events that really happen involves a value perspective. Any perspective cannot not yield both desired and undesired consequences. But recall that "desired" and "undesired" are arbitrary punctuations reflecting values. A different scenario may require a different perspective to be useful. Similarly, as mentioned earlier, the anticipated desired outcome from therapy may have rewards or reveal unanticipated consequences.

As applied to therapy, if one thinks in terms of Freudian psychology, as one observes a client and hears a client's story, one will probably interpret id, ego, superego, sibling rivalry, oedipal complex, libido, and more. These concepts and constructs are a real reality within the framework of Freudian psychology. And they become "real" in the therapy context. To therapists of a different theoretical persuasion, these phenomena do not exist, and thus they will not see them. The concept of a unicorn is real in Greek mythology, and one can have a meaningful conversation about them within this framework. One can have a meaningful conversation about id, ego, and superego, which are real in the framework of Freudian psychology. However, they have no real existence independent of this framework. No concept or construct has meaning or real existence independent of a framework. Similarly, "facts" set forth from a research project are framework relative. In a different research project based on a different theory, the "facts" from the first project can be equally valid and contradictory.

So, implicit in every social science theory is a set of values or "supposed to be" or "not supposed to be." This is true in the theories and stories of therapies at the level of simple cybernetics (Bowen, Satir, Minuchin, Nagy, Freud, Jung, Adler, Rogers, etc.) There are no value-neutral first-order theories. All theories for therapy at the level of simple cybernetics contain therapeutic procedures for helping the individual, marriage, or family become the way the theory suggests it should if it is to be normal or functional. Thus, all theories designed for therapy within a given culture or society will necessarily reflect the values implicit in the worldview of the society or culture of which therapists are members. In effect, therapists are sanctioned or licensed agents of the society of which they are members. In a sense, they are enforcers via facilitation—however, again a contradiction but only from the perspective of cybernetics of cybernetics. If higher-order cybernetics is the perspective of therapists, then they have no agenda about how people should be or what the successful outcome of therapy should be. That decision would be the clients' decisions (excluding immoral, illegal, or unethical outcomes, of course).

Let's focus once again on the two levels of systems theory or cybernetics—simple or first-order cybernetics or higher- or second-order cybernetics. Simple cybernetics or systems is the stuff of normative mental health practice utilizing the medical model. It is based on a science of "discovery" of what is "really out there" consistent with the philosophical traditions of modernism and structuralism. It is prescriptive in that it would describe individuals, marriages, and families that are normal relative to a specific standard of performance. It assumes that scientists and therapists as observers can observe without intruding or affecting the nature of the objects of observation. Simple cybernetics is similar to Newtonian physics, which believes in a clockwork universe and that by observation we can discover the basic building blocks of the universe, including understanding the people in it. That is, we punctuate ourselves outside the system we are observing. From an ecological perspective, this is akin to seeing *Homo sapiens* as not being part of nature. The assumption is that we can observe without influencing the dynamics of that which we are observing. That is, everything in this world is connected to everything else except us. Thus, in Seymour Sarason's (1981) view, we see ourselves *and* society rather than see ourselves *in* and a part of society. Therapy from this perspective has been and can be useful. It helped us develop "understandings" of families, communities, organizations, and nations. Of course, the understanding we developed was relative to the theory we used in our observations. But from the perspective of higher-order cybernetics, this view of seeing ourselves as independent observers may mask our participation in the creation of the problems that individuals, couples, families, and communities present for therapy by our observations.

Higher-order cybernetics or cybernetics of cybernetics addresses this inconsistency in the logic of systems theory from the perspective of first-order cybernetics. When assuming a totally interconnected universe, observers were excluding themselves as they "observed" and "discovered" what was "out there" in the system. They were acting as though they as "scientists" (observers, teachers, principals, therapists, parents) were not part of the world in which everything and everyone was connected. This difference is crucial. It seems that it all has to do with observation. To observe is to participate—become one with. In our attempts "to know" or have "knowledge," we punctuate ourselves outside that which we would understand. Alas, as mentioned earlier, we can never be outside that of which we are a part. Thus, even as we punctuate ourselves as a part of a system, we make this assertion from a position outside the system. Even when we look at ourselves doing things, there is a part of us that watches us doing them and another part of us watching ourselves watching the part of us that observes us doing things. Crazy making? Possibly, but it points to the limits of what we can know, and *ultimately what we can know is greatly influenced by what we already know and want to believe.* The realization of this dilemma, which has no solution, is what may keep us sane—if we use crazy or sane to categorize our experiences. This realization is what we believe Gregory Bateson (1972) described as having an epistemology that has a conscious awareness of itself.

Now, we turn to what is referred to as constructivism and social constructionism (postmodernism). Both perspectives introduce us to the concept of "story." It is important to remember that the worldviews of our societies are social constructions. Systems theory, constructivism, and even the concept of social constructionism are social constructions. In effect we invent theories (stories) in our attempts to explain ourselves to ourselves.

Constructivism is a skull-bound perspective. It asserts each of us has their personal understanding of the world. This understanding may or may not be consistent (and probably is a unique version) of the socially constructed stories that constitute the worldview or Weltanschauung of the society of which an individual (and therapist) is a member. Thus, both constructivism and social constructionism are about stories—the stories that individuals are socialized into as members of the society and their personal versions of the stories of the society. As Mair (1988) noted,

> Stories are habitations. We live in and through stories. They conjure worlds. We do not know the world other than as story world. Stories inform life. They hold us together and keep us apart. We inhabit the great stories of our culture. We live through stories. We are lived by the stories of our race and place. It is this enveloping and constituting function of stories that is especially important to sense more fully. We are, each of us, locations where the stories of our place and time become partially tellable. (p. 127)

Howard (1991) makes the following distinctions relative to stories: "Life—Stories We Live By; Psychopathology—Stories Gone Mad; Psychotherapy—Exercises in Story Repair" (p. 194).

If the stories people are telling themselves and are living their lives for are serving them well, and if people live their lives in the ways prescribed by their society, then there may be no reason for any form of therapy. If the stories provided by our culture or society are not serving people well, and as we shall see, many stories that live our lives for us are "crazy making," then the task of the therapist becomes a complementary role. Also, police officers and social workers become logical roles. The roles of each involve "helping" or enforcing people with *their* "problems of living" in the society. They have been described as the dirty workers of societies.

Believing that one is living their life in a story is a perspective that creates options. If a worldview includes the story that we live in stories rather than the way the world really is, then we have the option of seeking out and creating new stories through which we can live our lives. This perspective may well foster tolerance for people who live their lives in a different Weltanschauung or society. All societies socialize people into the socially constructed story of that society, but they are not socialized into the belief that the story into which they are being socialized is but a story. *That is, they do not have an epistemology that has a conscious awareness of itself.* And in most societies, the stories into which they are being socialized are often contradictory or paradoxical and often crazy making. And the stories of the society reflect basic values. When experience or behavior does not exhibit preferred values, problems may be experienced or observed by others. Bring on the therapists.

The bottom line of this is: *It's all made up.* And yet, *it is lived as real*—if you believe it to be real—and it will live your life for you. Our lives are intricately bound up with the stories we tell ourselves about ourselves, others, and our world. These stories live our lives for us. But almost all stories in our worldviews are stories about people out of context. Assessments of clients are all relative to the context of the assessment. According to the systems perspective, treatments should consider the contexts of our client systems, and the outcomes of therapy should consider the effects of the desired outcomes in the clients' lives.

Please note that problems are not constant across time. Different cultures will punctate different experiences or observed behaviors as problems. As values change, so that which people experience as problematic will change. Please note that in 1960, there were but 60 categories of disorders in the *DSM*. The most recent version of the *DSM* provides hundreds of diagnostic terms. Moreover, from the perspective of higher-order cybernetics, we professionals participate in creating the problems that people experience in their lives. The various *DSMs* are illustrative of this concept. Again, the "problems" you see and diagnose as a therapist are relative to the theory you use in your work with clients. They begin to experience the world through the language of the theory you use as you story or otherwise intervene in their lives. Thus, the theory or diagnosis lives their lives for them. This can be therapeutic or toxic. Please note also that the word *intervene* implies a position outside the system you are observing. If you take a higher-order systemic view, then you will see yourself as a part of the system, even before you see clients, and will use the word *perturb* or *intravene* rather than *intervene*. Also, please note that the observation that we are necessarily a part of the system is made from a perspective outside the system; hence, we observe ourselves observing ourselves being a part of the system.

Please note also that many problems that we experience are only problems when we compare ourselves or others compare us to the normative standards of how we are supposed to be. Many, if not most, of the problems that people experience derive from standards developed by social science and mental health professionals as agents of the society. And we professionals participate in the creation of the normative standards to which our clients compare each other and themselves. And comparing ourselves to others and others observing us (and correcting us) are integral to the process of socialization in any society.

We can live our lives in a constant state of tension as we experience problems based on values that are so utopian that they are impossible to obtain. William Schofield (1986) noted that we live in a cultural era in which not being free from anxiety and not being happy all the time are experienced as problematic. He also noted that social science and mental health professionals have a big investment in utopian notions like these. Utopian notions create clients and many dollars.

Dell (1983) reminds us that we don't treat problems; we treat values. Therapists are the keepers and enforcers of the culture's or society's values. These values and prescriptions for living up to these values can be and often are "crazy making."

From the systems perspective all therapy is relationship therapy, whether it is so conceptualized or not, because it assumes that problems can be solved in a relationship with a therapist. The concept of therapy implies relationship. Relationships are the "identified patients" in systemic approaches to therapy. Indeed, it is our assertion that as the individuals evolve symptomatic behavior referred to as disorders in the context of the family, so the families evolve that which is referred to as dysfunction in the context of the larger systems of which the family is a subsystem. The distinctions between levels of systems are our cuts in an interconnected universe in which there are no independent entities.

Therapists who view themselves working from the perspective of first- or second-order cybernetics can use concepts and processes from first-order systemic therapies as described previously. They may also use processes from individually focused therapies (Rogers, Jung, Adler, Glasser, behaviorism, etc.) but always with a focus on context and relationships rather than autonomous individuals with disorders. More generally speaking, there is no particular form that therapy or counseling needs to take. Any technique judged ethical by the community is allowable. They would also be observers of being participants-observers in their work. They also would have an awareness that believing is seeing rather than seeing is believing.

Relationships are everything—even life—especially life: "For it is the look on the face of the Other that gives us our sense of self" (Berkus, 1990).

Chapter 9

Requiem for Systemic Marital and Family Therapy

According to the *Oxford English Dictionary*, one definition of the word *requiem* is "an act or token of remembrance." The word *requiem* seems appropriate for the current status of *systemic* marital and family therapy. That which once flourished seems to be dead in the water in the current political, economic, and therapeutic climate. To us, marital and family therapy as a process and an orientation depends on the perspective on relationships that systems theory (particularly higher-order cybernetics) provides. Indeed, the very process of knowing (i.e., drawing distinctions) necessarily involves relationships. No entity we have distinguished from another entity is meaningful without the other. Living necessarily involves connection and relationship. But we get ahead of ourselves. We wish to tell our story about how the movement away from systemic marital and family therapy happened and explore the possibility of a resurrection.

As we look back over the evolution of systems theory in the field of mental health in general and family therapy in particular, we find that initially there was great excitement, with metaphoric brass bands, the waving of flags, and cheers for the paradigm shift it described (Becvar & Becvar, 2013). Systems theory seemed to offer renewed hope for the resolution of persistent intrapersonal and interpersonal problems. Salvador Minuchin reflected this optimism when he stated,

> Family therapy will take over psychiatry in one or two decades, because it is about man in context. It is a therapy that belongs to our century, while individual therapy belongs to the nineteenth century. This is not a pejorative. It is simply that things evolve and change, and during any historical period certain ways of looking at life and responding to life begin to crop up everywhere. Family therapy is to psychiatry what Pinter is to theatre and ecology is to natural science. (in Malcolm, 1978, p. 41)

But alas, the blossoming of systems theory was very brief, and the fruit borne appears to be withering on the vine. Shields et al. (1994) refer to this issue as the marginalization of family therapy. Hoyt and Gurman (2012) ponder the future of the practice of therapy with more than one person when they write, "Wither Couple/Family Therapy" (p. 13). Marriage and family therapists (MFTs) won the legal battle in Texas over the right to diagnose using the individually focused *DSM* (Morris, 2017). Some celebrated this as a victory, but one might say, "With another victory like this, we systemic therapists are done for." Morris (2017) wrote,

> [T]he core practice of seeing whole families together in therapy has become an exception rather than the general rule. Breunlin and Jacobsen (2014) estimate, based on practice pattern data, that MFTs see whole families less than 10% of the time. The authors ask, "Why have we been so willing to forfeit one of our signature ideas that the context for problems and their resolutions is often the whole family?" (p. 10)

In addition, during a variety of conference presentations, we have heard discussions of classical psychodynamic, intrapsychic therapy approaches that use the language of systems theory to describe the model but are not systemic from our perspective. The approaches described in these presentations are not unusual, especially relative to agency work and often in private practice, where MFTs manage to survive by abandoning much of their education and training as they negotiate the economics of professional practice.

It is our view that systems theory as the language of the seminal theory for the practice of marital and family therapy may be alive, but systemic marital and family therapy is dying. We therefore offer our "Requiem for Systemic Marital and Family Therapy." However, by offering our requiem, we may also open the door and hope for its future. The basic concepts of systems theory will not go away. There is nowhere in this world that one can stand and not be a part of the world. Attempts to know and understand people and their problems in living out of context is like trying to understand a fish by studying it in a frying pan (Minuchin, 1984). Also, perhaps we will again see discourses about epistemology that have been curiously absent in recent MFT and other professional literature. We believe that all forms of therapy have an epistemological foundation and that these foundations should be articulated and discussed. As Gregory Bateson (1972) noted, people should have a conscious awareness of the epistemologies that guide their lives. Indeed, we hope this chapter is controversial enough to open up conversations about epistemology, aesthetics, and pragmatics of systemic therapy and its future. But first, it is important to share our story about how systems theory became marginalized and allowed to wither.

Whereof do we speak? In their efforts to become a distinct mental health profession, in their efforts to seek validation through certification and licensure, to obtain credibility along with other mainstream practitioners, and to obtain third-party payments as a legitimate mental health provider, family therapists inevitably moved away from the basic tenets of the holistic, unifying metatheory that initially offered a way to transcend artificial distinctions within the social sciences and mental health professions. The requirement for evidence-based "treatments" for *DSM*-diagnosed problems typically locates the problem within the individual with almost no consideration of context, and typically the diagnostician (observer) has no conscious awareness of diagnosing with no regard for context. This practice tends to reify the word assigned to the set of symptoms observed in the diagnosis. What is interesting is that by implementing an "evidence-based" treatment, the therapist's behavior with the client is a change in context with no reference to systemic dialogue about how an existing context participates in maintaining the symptomatic behavior. Ah, but once again, we get ahead of ourselves.

How did this happen? Like any seed, the seed of systems theory needed to fall on fertile ground in order to flourish. Seeds that fall among rocks, briars, or thistles will not germinate and grow. Systems theory has not flourished, for it has not found fertile ground in the context of Western ideology. Indeed, it is contradictory to Western ideology and its related political and economic systems of which the various mental health fields are an integral part. It does not fit the narrative story and the traditions of Western society. Typically, discourses by theorists and therapists about clinical practice and "mental health" problems are made as though the theorists and practitioners are not a part of the society. That is, they tend to view themselves *and* society rather than see themselves *in* or a part of society (Sarason, 1981). In contrast to higher-order cybernetics, which requires that we see ourselves *in* the society, they do not see themselves as participating in creating the problems they subsequently treat in therapy. This viewpoint seems to assume that problems are spontaneously generated within clients rather than having evolved in the social context of the society of which theorists and therapists are a part.

Many philosophical and practical aspects of systems theory make clear the conflict we see. First, systems theory does not address the problems and issues described by various political groups in a way that satisfies these political groups. Systems theory provides only a perspective on the problem and reminds us of the environmental fallacy (Churchman, 1979). That is, every problem reflects a value perspective and has an environment that, unless taken into consideration, not only may not solve the problem but also may give rise to more serious problems. Systems theory thus suggests that we examine the assumptions and values we punctuate in defining a problem as a problem. It would have us file an environmental impact statement before any solution is attempted. In one sense, it is too powerful, and in another sense, it is impotent for immediate resolution of the problems defined by society. Systems theory does not give us noble causes, dragons to slay, or protagonists to fight. In other words, second-order cybernetics would help us be self-conscious of the epistemologies that underlie that which is defined as problematic and in need of solution. This necessarily involves our looking in a mirror and seeing ourselves looking in a mirror—seeing ourselves participating in both the creation of problems in need of solution and the subsequent resolution of these problems.

The mandate of our society would have us locate problems within the individual rather than in the context of which the individual is a part. To reiterate, this mandate also encourages us to see ourselves *and* the society rather than to see ourselves *in* the society (Sarason, 1981). In our view, the mental health field is badly in need of therapy—a therapy that would help us see that we are an integral part of creating the very problems we subsequently "treat." Indeed, in our view, the systems perspective would suggest a need for conceptual therapy for our theories of therapy. Of course, this conceptual therapy is only needed from the perspective of higher-order cybernetics.

Systems theory thus has rightly been accused of being apolitical, amoral, a-aesthetic, and areligious (Churchman, 1979). Without values, there are no problems in need of therapy. Therapeutic theories evolve with a society or culture in order to serve people with the problems as defined by that society or culture. Accordingly, the classic, pragmatic, systemic family therapy theories of Satir, Minuchin, Nagy, and Bowen describe dynamics of family dysfunction and family health within the Western culture or society. Higher-order cybernetics does not espouse a particular social order or arrangement. That which is defined as an anomaly within a culture or society is not viewed as an anomaly from the higher-order systems perspective. It logically fits and is a role that fits the context. It makes an important difference to a therapist and therapy if the "symptomatic behavior" is viewed not as an anomaly but as a logical role in the social context. Symptomatic behavior is adaptive. Jay Haley (1976) suggested that symptoms evolve to influence relationships.

Systems theory also presents a conceptual challenge to the practice of social science research. If one thinks systemically, then it becomes inconsistent to do research in the traditions of logical positivism and empiricism. Systems theory suggests that as researchers we cannot just observe—that by our observations we intrude, we perturb, and we transform the participants in our research. Quantum physics became aware of this phenomenon as early as the 1920s. This is the uncertainty principle. Lewis Thomas (1979) describes this phenomenon in quantum physics:

The uncertainty principle doesn't mean that the observer necessarily destroys the precise momentum or shifts the particle, in the act of observing, although these things happen. The observer and his apparatus *create* the reality to be observed. Without him, there are all sorts of possibilities for single particles, in all sorts of wave patterns. The reality to be studied by his instruments is not simply there, it is brought into existence by the laboratory. (p. 71)

Heinz von Foerster (in Wolf, 1998) offers a similar observation about an epistemological problem as he describes the move from first- to second-order cybernetics:

(i) Observations are not absolute but relative to the observer's point of view (i.e. his coordinate system: Einstein); (ii) Observations affect the observed so as to obliterate the observer's hope for prediction (i.e. his uncertainty is absolute: Heisenberg). After this, we are now in the possession of the truism that a description (of the universe) implies one who describes (observes it). (pp. 56–57)

Thus, participants in social science research are self-consciously observing themselves participating in the research project. As observers of their participation, perhaps the participants in our research should take part in the development of the theories that evolve from our research. They may be able to explain their social and personal experiences better than do researchers who conceptually view themselves as viewers from outside. The classical study by Caplan and Nelson (1973) illustrates this effect. It reminds us that we cannot be separate from that of which we are necessarily a part. Indeed, that of which we are a part has no outside for us and is a credo of second-order cybernetics. We are accustomed to a science that allows us to view ourselves as separate from and objective observers of the phenomena we study. Systems theory insists we include ourselves in the equation and be responsible for the effects of research on participants.

In writing this chapter, we become consciously aware of a philosophical dilemma. The statement that we necessarily belong to systems that for us have no outside (we are inside and one with them) is made from a perspective "outside" the system of which we are necessarily a part. That is, by asserting "we are one with," we also are describing our belonging from a perspective "outside" the system. Indeed, the concept of observation necessarily includes self-observation as well as observation of one's observation of self. The assertion that we are part of the system is made from a perspective outside the system, which is consistent but also contradictory.

Systems theory would have us see circular causality, reciprocity, and recursion. Instead of "seeing is believing," we must espouse a "believing is seeing" perspective. From a systems perspective, we would see relationships between people as the primary units of analysis rather than focusing on the isolated monad. We would see our clients not as they are independent of context but as they are with us the way we are with them—the context of our observation and participation. We would be aware that if we give our clients a *DSM* diagnosis, then we are providing them with an identity that may take precedence over other words that might describe them equally well. Indeed, the word in the diagnosis may override all other words that describe a life: "You refer to yourself as bipolar. I wonder if you are anything else."

Moreover, in many cases, the *DSM* diagnosis is often a life sentence, as people in our clients' lives relate to diagnosis in a way that logically complements and maintains the very behavior that was the basis for the diagnosis. A basic systemic concept is that no behavior can maintain itself on its own energy. It needs a logical complement (Wátzlawick et al., 1974). We don't relate to people; we relate to the stories we tell ourselves about people. In essence, the diagnosis may live peoples' lives for them and requires the social context of which the "diagnosis" is a part to adapt or accommodate and thus maintain the symptoms that were the basis for the diagnosis. The perspective of psychiatrist Irvin Yalom (2015) makes an important observation regarding *DSM* diagnoses.

> We have come to believe that the contortions we psychotherapists must go through to meet the demands of insurance companies for precise diagnoses are detriments to both therapist and patient. In the diagnostic procedure, we are not carving at the joints of nature. Diagnostic categories are invented and arbitrary: They are a product of committee vote and invariably undergo considerable revision with each passing decade. The chore of making a formal diagnosis is more than a simple nuisance. It may, in fact, *impede* our work by obscuring, even negating, the full-bodied, multidimensional individual facing us in our office (p. 181).

Luhrmann (2015) offered another perspective on *DSM* diagnoses:

> Our current diagnostic system—the main achievement of the biomedical revolution in psychiatry—drew a sharp, clear line between those who were sick and those who were well, and that line was determined by science. The system started with the behavior of persons, sorted them into types. That approach sank deep roots into our culture, possibly because sorting ourselves into different kinds of people comes naturally to us. . . . The British Psychological Association rejects the centrality of diagnosis for seemingly quite different reasons—among them, because defining people by a devastating label may not help them. (p. 5)

Is the *DSM* scientific? An observation by Roach (2017) provides a partial answer to this question: "Making diagnoses in psychiatry can be difficult. There isn't a lab test or imaging study to confirm the diagnosis, and the symptoms people notice can overlap among several different conditions" (p. 4).

Given the awareness of the problem of diagnosis, systemic therapists would need to abandon the individualistic stories invented to explain what is happening when therapy is not going well. Such stories include "The client is resistant"; "The client does not want to change"; "The client is not motivated"; "The client is in denial." By contrast, if we were to be consistent with second-order cybernetics, then we would include ourselves in the equation. To be consistent with the systems framework, it would be more appropriate to say something like, "How vividly do I describe myself when I feel my client to be resistant?" If we view the relationship between therapist and client as a recursive dance, then when therapists label their clients, they must also give themselves a complementary label. They cannot exclude themselves, and together their clients and they maintain each other in their complementary relationship. The systems paradigm would also require therapists to view symptomatic behavior in context. The client's symptomatic behavior may be perceived as serving an important purpose. Therapists would not see symptomatic behavior as an anomaly but behavior that logically fits contexts. Indeed, clients with systemically oriented therapists would begin to experience themselves in context.

The systems perspective does not encourage the search for "underlying causes" of problems, an integral part of Western mental health practice, theory, and research (i.e., linear cause-effect thinking). While we may be able to create a story about a historical basis (a why) for a current interactional pattern, systems theory does not seek the why that is so near and dear to us and is such an important part of our Western ideology and the early practice of psychotherapy in the tradition of Newtonian physics. Moreover, the search for "cause" of problems typically involves linear thinking in that "cause" necessarily is in the past (Capra, 1983). There are many historical whys available in the therapy literature. The systemic concept of equifinality suggests that no matter how we got here, no matter what story we use to explain our journey to here and now, this is where we are. Thus, what maintains a problem takes precedence over what caused a problem. Systems theory suggests that there are no causes that we can know with certainty. To see a particular cause or causes, one must think linearly (i.e., billiard-ball causality). Systems theory would have us see circularity and recursion, and if pushed to causality, it would have us see reciprocal causality. Its language would include the what, the when, and the how but not the historical why.

Our culture separates mind from body and cognition from affect and behavior. Systems theory provides a unifying perspective that avoids these distinctions and allows us to see mind and body as one as well as the integration of cognition, affect, and behavior. Indeed, the assertion that there is a biological or chemical component in "mental illness" often does not include the possibility that context may be a factor in the biological or chemical component. Indeed, even offering hereditary or genetic explanations does not preclude contextual contributions to that which is described as "dysfunctional."

Systems theory would also have us see an integrated self and system that does not punctuate a boundary for ourselves at our skin. Western ideology would have people experience themselves as separate from the context of which they are an integral part. Rather, as Alan Watts (1972) noted,

> Self is the whole cosmos centered around the particular time, place, and activity called John Doe. Thus the soul is not in the body, but the body in the soul, and the soul is the entire network of relationships and processes which make up your environment, and apart from which you are nothing. . . . The only true atom is the universe. (pp. 62–63)

Of course, this concept challenges the promise of rewards and threats of punishments that are central to social control processes used in Western ideologies.

Haley (1976) makes us aware of another important issue if we think systemically: that of therapists working with an individual. He noted that we must be concerned with helping not only the client but also those who cannot not be affected by changes in our client. Such reverberations are inevitable if we view people as interconnected and individual symptoms as a part of a relationship contract between and among people in our clients' lives.

Systems theory is particularly troublesome to professionals who like to feel that we play an important part in solving society's problems. Indeed, it is often difficult for those of us who are idealistic and highly motivated to solve human problems to consider the possibility that we may be a part of the problem of an ever-increasing number of clients with problems to solve. Sarason (1981) called attention to this issue when he noted that psychologists tend to see themselves *and* the society rather than see themselves *in* the society. By seeing themselves as independent observers of the society, therapists can seduce themselves into believing that the problems we attempt to solve exist "out there," independent of our participation.

However, Schofield (1986) noted that social science professionals have a great influence in the defining range of "normalcy" that people experience in their lives. Schofield noted that a liberal definition of *mental illness* would have more people experience themselves as having problems, while a conservative definition of *mental illness* would have fewer people experiencing themselves as having problems. Interestingly but not surprisingly, the number of people with problems in need of therapeutic solution reflects the number of mental health therapists available to provide this service. The more therapists available, the more probable is a liberal definition of *mental illness* or *family dysfunction*. This is a supply-and-demand issue. In this case, the supply of therapists creates its own demands. Of course, this is only an issue from the perspective of higher-order systems theory or cybernetics.

By making us aware of the participation of therapists and other social scientists as described here, the systems perspective reminds us that by setting unrealistically high standards for individuals, families, and society in our therapeutic and prevention models, we may provide people with information for a constant state of dissonance as they attempt to implement these models into their lives. Schofield (1986) noted that we live in a cultural epoch in which the failure to be free from anxiety and not be happy all the time is pathological. The "supposed to be's and do's" that people experience and over which we professionals have some control can increase the probability that many normal developmental crises will be experienced as problems in need of solutions. Many of the experiences of events in life can be described as traumatic. However, therapists could help people feel free to experience the existential anxiety of uncertainty and the search for meaning and purpose without construing the event as traumatic. Life happens.

Systems theory reminds us that we play an important role in influencing the way people experience themselves as just described. At another level, we help to create issues and problems to solve by the research we conduct and publish. The content of professional journals inevitably filters out to the popular press. Research results often become the rationale for implementing particular social policies as well as becoming selective grist for political mills. Indeed, efforts to prevent problems very probably create a sensitivity to them and bring forth the very problem we seek to prevent. Again, we cannot just observe; the very process of observing and communicating our observations and our concerns cannot not have an effect on individuals and the social systems of which they are a part. Western ideology would focus on fixing people rather than the context to which they belong.

So where does this leave us? The roles of professional "mental health" practitioners in Western societies are socially sanctioned and legally regulated. These sanctions and regulations require professional practice consistent with the ideology and politics of these societies. Economic rewards are awarded to those who practice and conduct research within the boundaries of the prevailing ideology. Consistent with this reality, medical-model professional practice based on the *DSM* is required and is alive and well. Thus, the systems perspective is marginalized. And yet, a systems perspective will not go away. Epistemologically, it is only *one* perspective, and yet it rears its head whenever we attempt to do only one thing and find that other things are affected and change in ways we had not anticipated with our limited vision. This experienced "reality" of a totally interconnected universe suggests that it must be accommodated in our therapeutic models and practice. Indeed, if we are to be a part of the solution to increased incidence of "mental illness" and "family dysfunction," then we must include a self-conscious awareness of the context in which "mental illness" is a logical role and not an anomaly. Also, we must be self-consciously aware that we may be a part of the problem. This self-conscious awareness as being part of the problem also opens the possibility that we can be a part of the solution.

Indeed, in fairness to therapists and students of marital and family therapy (counseling, social work, psychology), it is important that they be knowledgeable about work within the paradigm of normative, mental health practice consistent with the modernist philosophical and research tradition. This received view in the social sciences is the "knowledge" they will be expected to demonstrate when they assume positions in agencies or private practice and when they take their licensing exams. In essence, they must be prepared to demonstrate that they have been appropriately socialized into the received view of their particular professional identity. They must learn about diagnosis and the world of psychoactive drugs. The accreditation agencies and licensing boards stand in judgment about whether graduate programs educating students have the structures in place to ensure that the socialization of the profession is appropriate.

As noted throughout, this world is the world dictated by the ideology of the society, psychiatry, and the diagnostic categories of the *DSM*. However, a part of their socialization into using the categories of the *DSM* is to view the categories as "real" things and not as metaphors or constructs assigned to patterns of behavior. It is, after all, a *Diagnostic and Statistical Manual*, and because it is statistical, it must be scientific, and therefore it describes "real" phenomena. And once an assignment to a category has been made, there is the expectation that standardized and validated (evidence-based using traditional research protocols) treatment protocols must be followed.

However, therapists must also remember that the *DSM* is a social construction. It provides a common language for dialogue between professionals about our clients. Dialogues using other socially constructed languages are available and may be more benign and helpful than a *DSM* diagnosis. Other "evidence-based treatments" (including systemic therapies) for problems in living with self and others are available and could be used. However, treatment protocols for relationships are rarely, if ever, accepted for third-party payments. Indeed, well-trained systemic MFTs may find their fluency in the languages of systemic therapy wash out in the context of the language of individually based diagnostics required for professional practice. Particularly, this may be the case for therapists who work in agency settings. Therapists in private practice may have more options.

The scenarios described here may make the resurrection of systemic marital and family therapy quite difficult, if not impossible. Indeed, survival for systemically based therapy may require a double-consciousness. Members of minority cultures become quite adept in developing different languages and different behavior protocols when they attempt to survive in a larger society that defines a different appropriate protocol to be a member of the society. They learn the game, and they learn to play the game. Of course, they must never announce that they know the game and are playing the game. If they were to do so, then they would be more marginalized and perhaps ostracized.

As mentioned earlier, therapists in private practice may have more freedom to do systemically informed therapy. They are in a position to speak the language of the *DSM*-informed therapy and the language of relationally informed systemic therapy. Indeed, conversations with clients about the difference between the two paradigms and consequences of therapy informed by each can be an important dialogue. However, even this may be challenging because most clients have internalized and may be at least somewhat informed about the categories of the *DSM*. And, if they wish to be reimbursed for their therapy, then a *DSM* diagnosis may be requested.

LAST RITES OR RESURRECTION?

We began this exploration with the following statement about our focus: We wish to tell our story about how the movement away from systemic marital and family therapy happened and explore the possibility of a resurrection. Having addressed the first part of our story, the time has come to consider the second part: the possibility of resurrection. For this we can only point out some things to consider and offer our speculations. We note particularly that change is inevitable. However, according to the concept of stochastic processes, although change may be inevitable, we can't predict with certainty what the change will look like.

Systems theory and family therapy were borne out of efforts in several areas, including studies of the technology of war, research on human communication with a particular focus on schizophrenia, and clinical explorations relative to shifting from individual to interpersonal interactions. *The goal was never to create a separate mental health profession.* However, over time, that became our focus as models were created, schools of family therapy drew excited followers, and the effectiveness of new ways of thinking was described and demonstrated. The systems perspective did not find a home with other established mental health professions. Old professional associations were revised, new professional associations were created, and the quest for recognition was underway. This pursuit was so successful that MFTs are now licensable in all 50 states, licensed in Canada, and are being recognized in other countries through International Family Therapy Association (IFTA).

The quest for recognition was primarily about equality in the workplace and the need for MFTs to be able to find jobs and be reimbursable by third-party payers. This certainly was a reasonable goal. However, what we wanted was recognition within a system whose philosophical orientation was diametrically opposed to our systemic orientation, especially at the level of second-order cybernetics. Accordingly, we would have to know and use the categories of the *DSM*. We would have to demonstrate the ability to diagnose and treat mental disorders. In other words, we would have to be inconsistent with our basic belief system—that which is unique about how we think and what we do in our efforts to help our clients. Perhaps seeing no way around this dilemma, that is what we chose to do.

Was there another path we might have taken or that we might take now? While unlikely to occur, we believe there is and that so doing might enable us to resurrect systemic marital and family therapy at the levels of both first-order and second-order cybernetics. For example, we have found, in our many years of clinical experience, that one of the best sources of referrals is satisfied clients. That, of course, means that we must be conscientious in our efforts to be effective. We can create educational and supervisory experiences that enable students and supervisees to be successful in their work with clients. We can be more sensitive to the language we use with clients given our focus on relationships and the need to be respectful at all times. We can free up precious workspace, given that we do not need to spend great periods of time dealing with third-party payers. We can offer a flexible-fee scale and still receive compensation comparable to what the third-party payers are likely to provide.

If enough of us refused to buy into the current system, then we could operate in a manner that is consistent with our systemic orientation. Is this just a silly pipe dream? Probably. Could it work? Over time, it probably could. Unfortunately, if we don't try something of this sort, if we stay on our current path, then we surely will get where we are going: We become one more mental health profession in the Western ideological tradition. In that case, this submission may be best understood as the last rites for a powerful opportunity.

Chapter 10

The Ecosystemic Story

Implications for Therapists

According to Ricoeur (1978) and Watts (1972), any person born to a society or culture is socialized into the worldview, paradigm, or narrative story of that culture or society. Similarly, professional therapists, social workers, psychologists, and psychiatrists are socialized into the narrative story of their particular professions. Further, the narrative story of each profession fits the culture or society in which the professional is being trained to function (Sarason, 1981).

By contrast, the ecosystemic paradigm, or second-order cybernetics (G. Bateson, 1979; Keeney, 1983; Maturana, 1975; Varela, 1979; von Foerster, 1981), assumes recursion, complementarity, and circular causality; focuses on relationships, context, and wholeness; embraces the notion that reality is perceptual, subjective, and constructed; and acknowledges theoretical relativity (Becvar & Becvar, 2013). It also includes as part of its socialization process an awareness that one is being socialized into a paradigm and that this paradigm is but a story about stories and about being socialized into a story about stories. These differences define the ecosystemic paradigm as countercultural and thus as having far-reaching implications for the practice of mental health therapy.

Because we cannot "really" know what is going on "out there," we invent stories, which vary from cultures and societies. All the stories, to greater or lesser degrees, are valid for the purposes for which they were invented. Second-order cybernetics is thus about stories and about the stories we tell ourselves to describe our relationship with things, other creatures, other people, and ourselves. Indeed, even a story that does not assume an interconnection with things, other creatures, and other people is seen as describing a particular kind of connection with these phenomena. That is, the stories people tell themselves about a particular thing, creature, or person also describes how they will and must relate to that thing, creature, or person (including themselves) if they are to experience coherence and consistency within themselves. For example, the biblical "dominion over" story regarding other creatures and things in the world stands in contrast to a "stewardship" story, and one will behave very differently as a function of which story one accepts. Similarly, the "man should be the head of the household story" stands in contrast to the "equality of gender roles" story, and its proponents will behave in significantly different ways.

Thus, the stories we tell ourselves constitute our experienced reality. What exists "out there" for us depends on our framework of concepts and constructs. The stories we tell ourselves inevitably define our relationships with others in our world. By virtue of acting in a manner consistent with these stories, we create the reality (i.e., the characteristics in the other that our story describes). This is Gregory Bateson's (1979) "mind in nature." As he wrote in the introduction to *Steps to an Ecology of Mind* (1972),

> The questions which this book raises are ecological. How do ideas interact? Is there some sort of natural selection which determines the survival of some ideas and the extinction or death of others? What sort of economics limits the multiplicity of ideas in a given region of mind? What are the necessary conditions for stability (or survival) of such a system or subsystem? (pp. xv–xvi)

From this perspective, there are no distorted perceptions. All stories are but perceptions of a world we can never know in an absolute sense inasmuch as we do not have a god's-eye view of the universe (Bronowski, 1978). No story is inherently superior to another. Each story serves the purposes for which it was invented more or less well. Each person's story is unique and has not been told in exactly the same way by anyone else.

Ricoeur (1978) suggests that the therapist's task is to help clients tell stories that provide coherence, meaning, and purpose in their lives. The second-order cybernetics dimension that we would add suggests that therapists help clients become aware, either implicitly or explicitly, that the stories they tell themselves necessarily define their relationships with people (including themselves), creatures, and things. People, creatures, and things do not interact. As Gregory Bateson (1972) also noted, rather, the ideas that we have about people, creatures, and things interact. Plas (1986) wrote,

> The absolute one, true reality of life can never be an important issue from a systemic point of view. Rather, it is recognized that a multiplicity of tales is possible. What is important are meaningful wholes, descriptions of the patterns that guide movement. Since . . . we cannot have access to ultimate absolute reality, our challenge becomes one of seeing relationships, of knitting together incoherent parts. (pp. 81–82)

As we talk of stories rather than "reality," we are reminded that it is not possible anywhere or anytime to speak truth in the positivist, Western sense of that term. The truth we speak from a systemic point of view is a contextual truth. A piece of the puzzle (or dynamic of the plot) is true if it fits, if it helps to complete the pattern from which emerges meaning.

IMPLICATIONS FOR THERAPISTS

As mentioned earlier, second-order cybernetics constitutes a revolution or a countercultural movement in contradistinction to the paradigm into which most mental health therapists have been socialized. According to Kuhn (1970), however, professionals who have an investment in a specific paradigm do not easily give up that paradigm. In the same way, clients have an investment in their own personal paradigm, or worldview, which they began to develop early in their lives and to which they have added throughout their lives. While one can assume that that this personal paradigm is no longer serving them as well as they thought it would (or else they would not be presenting themselves for therapy), it is all they know. It is their reality. It is their personal version of the worldview of their society. With this introduction, let us venture to consider how we would deal with such a situation, or to view the practice of mental health therapy according to a second-order cybernetics perspective:

1. The client (individual, couple, or family) is telling a unique story. If the client is a couple or family, then you will hear a different story from each member. There are as many different couples or families as there are members. Each story has its own coherence and will probably have a coherence with the stories of other couple or family members.

2. Therapists are not diagnosticians. They do not think in terms of pathology or health. They do not use the language of deficit or disorder. They see coherence, logic, and normalcy in the context of the other and the stories each tells themselves about the other. The sequence of diagnosis, treatment planning, and treatment gives way to a process of dialogue or dialectic (a recursive dance) between the therapist and the client. Therapists are not the experts, although the therapy context and the client's beliefs about that context may punctuate therapists as experts.

3. Because therapists do not diagnose, they probably will not use psychometric instruments. To do so would be to impose on clients the story on which the instrument is based, which would inevitably become part of the clients' experienced realities. No instrument discovers what is "really" going on except within the values, theories, or stories that

guided the development of that particular instrument. The title, items, and scales that logically fit the meaning or value system underlying the instrument selected for assessment or research give clients in therapy or subjects in research a particular way of experiencing themselves. Moreover, they cannot not be affected by the process of completing the instrument.

4. Therapists and researchers are not discoverers; they are shapers and cocreators (with clients) of human experience. Therapists are qualitative instruments who also cannot know or discover what is "really" going on. The questions therapists ask, the components of clients' stories that therapists select for paraphrase or empathy, lead clients to tell their stories in a particular way. Stories told are relative to the context: that is, relative to the audience. Thus, the story a client tells to an Adlerian therapist will be different from that told to a therapist with a Rogerian or Jungian orientation. From this perspective, the kinds of problems clients "need" to solve in order to alleviate their problems will be the clients' stories as amended by the therapists' theoretical orientations.

5. Therapists operating from the perspective of second-order cybernetics are aware that (1) they cannot not behave, (2) they cannot not communicate, and (3) they cannot not influence the direction of the therapy. They are, however, more likely to be guided by clients (client-centered) rather than a received-view theory (theory-centered). They are likely to view therapy as a recursive dance between client and therapist who together coevolve an alternative story that provides solutions that the client's original story did not. Milton Erickson noted in personal communication in 1979, "People come with problems they cannot solve; I give them problems they can solve." Thus, the client and therapist coevolve a different story that fits the client's original story and that (1) may define the problem differently, (2) may define the presenting problem as not a problem, or (3) may suggest that the "attempted solution" to the presenting problem is the problem (Wátzlawick et al., 1974).

6. The therapist and the client may cocreate a different story that may contain aspects of any of the received-view stories from classical theories of therapy and personality or theories of family therapy. As a second-order cybernetician, the therapist does not discriminate against any story and believes that each story has potential utility for the client. The test for the utility of a story is not on the truth or falseness of the story but on appropriateness for the client. Thus, the therapist may appear to be Freudian, Jungian, Adlerian, Ellisian, Rogerian, Bowenian, or Minuchian. However, for the therapist, the issue is not one of the truth

of the particular story but its utility for that particular client. This utility is also the second-order cybernetician's aesthetic.

7. Therapists do not view their clients as "resistant," "not motivated," "not wanting to change," or "in denial." If the therapists punctuate the client as being "resistant," then they must include themselves in consideration of what is going on. Resistance is viewed as a relational phenomenon and may be seen as an attempt by the therapist to impose a story on the client that either does not fit the client or is ill-timed. Clients provide the cues about how they can be helped. Ecosystemic therapists are more sensitive to these cues than they are to theories that suggest how and at what pace therapy should progress. Erickson noted that he invented a different theory for each client. The theories or stories therapists use to understand their clients must evolve to fit and respect (another aesthetic and an ethic) the unique life situation of each client.

8. The therapist probably does not use the *DSM* or any other standard diagnostic protocol. From the perspective of second-order cybernetics, "Psychiatric diagnoses exist only in the eye of the observer. Worse yet, diagnoses, because they carry attributions of causality and hence blame, act to reinforce the problems they are meant to benevolently explain" (Boscolo et al., 1987, pp. 14–15). The therapist views the *DSM* as a system of thinking based on a particular kind of story consistent with normative mental health practice in our culture. The therapist would view using such a system as participation in the maintenance of the problem.

9. Therapists are very careful about their choice of words or metaphors to describe clients' situations. Therapists are aware that because they are viewed by clients as experts, their stories will strongly influence the creation of a reality for clients. Therefore, therapists are more likely to normalize rather than to pathologize. Indeed, if the clients' stories are heard, including their perception of the context in which they live, therapists will hear normalcy. This is not normalcy in the sense of an observer outside the system using some statistical standard of normal grief, normal anger, normal anxiety, and so on but as making sense given the clients' stories and contexts. Rather, therapists are likely to normalize the clients' experiences when the therapists hear the clients apply a statistical normal or a normal that they have observed for other people relative to themselves. Perceived deviations from statistical standards of normalcy may be reframed as the clients' uniqueness and as a necessary difference. Many clients experience problems when they apply standards to themselves that do not fit their unique circumstances.

10. Given the fact that the concepts of "denial" and "resistance" are not consistent with this perspective, therapists do not confront. If therapists

see clients as "in denial" or "resistant," then they are describing a problem in the way in which the client and therapist are dancing together. In this case, the therapist considers another approach to help facilitate a better fit. Among the questions therapists might privately ask themselves are, "What story am I telling myself about this client?" and "What alternative story would be more likely to fit and be useful to the client?" A collaborative question to be addressed with the client is, "We seem to be stuck and not dancing well together. What do you see going on? What do you think would be helpful?" The latter question would be more consistent with the recursive ecosystemic perspective. The former would be more consistent with the medical model of therapist as expert who "treats."

11. Therapists are aware that any change made by clients must influence the clients' relationships with others in their families or social networks. Thus, an ethical issue for therapists is a concern for the others who will inevitably be affected by the changes in clients. Further, there is an awareness that if the changes requested by clients were to occur, then they might not necessarily be experienced as "good" if their networks of relationships are affected adversely. You can't do just one thing. Each requested change deserves an exploration by the therapist and client of its potential environmental impact. Each solution reveals different problems.

12. Ecosystemic therapists are aware that solving one problem may give rise to higher-order problems (Keeney, 1983). Because ecosystemic therapists see all people, creatures, and things as interconnected, they may see a "wisdom" in that which is viewed as a problem. Ecosystemic therapists may tell themselves the story that the problem evolved in a network or relationships and "fits" or is "coherent" in clients' networks or relationships. Indeed, the "problem" may be a solution to a different problem. If the original problem is solved, then other problems may be a logical consequence. Again, therapists collaborate with clients to develop an environmental-impact statement. For example, being abused as a wife may be less of a problem than the problems of loneliness, homelessness, or poverty that might follow separation or divorce. Thus, solving the problem of spouse abuse involves solving many other problems that necessarily follow from solving the presenting problem. Therapists are aware that you cannot do one thing. They are ethically required to inform clients that they cannot do just one thing. Every solution has its own unique problems.

13. To ecosystemic therapists, the paradoxical injunction is not a trick or a con and poses no particular ethical problem. A paradox is only a paradox from a frame of reference that defines it as illogical and thus

paradoxical. You can only view it as a trick or a con if you believe you know what is "really" going on or know the truth. This ecosystemic therapists cannot know. Restraint from change or prescribing the symptom makes perfect sense from a frame of reference that sees the problem as a solution to another problem or sees consequences from the changes that may adversely affect clients' relationships with others. Following the lead of Virginia Satir (1967), for example, depression or anxiety are not necessarily problematic. The problem is the conscious attempt not to be depressed or anxious, the "be spontaneous" paradox (Wátzlawick et al., 1974). Such efforts give rise to being depressed about one's depression or anxious about one's anxiety. Thus, it is the higher-order feelings about one's feelings that are the problem, not the first-level feelings. Prescribing the symptom of consciously trying to feel depressed or anxious is an attempt to normalize the first-level feeling by framing it as a normal response. Similarly, giving it a positive connotation or describing a wisdom in the symptom may preclude other, perhaps even more serious problems. Restraint from change makes sense for the client whose urgency to solve the problem may be the problem.

14. For ecosystemic therapists, mental health is relationship health. The kind of relationships people experience are relative to the stories they tell themselves about self, others, creatures, and things. There is no objective reality out there that we can know. What is "out there" for us is an ecology of ideas about what is out there (G. Bateson, 1972).

15. Therapists do not view therapy as praxis. They do not have a particular value or political agenda for their clients and no investment in a way a person, marriage, or family should be. Indeed, to have a value or political agenda would be an ethical dilemma. Amendments to this statement include outcomes that are immoral, abusive, or unethical.

16. Believing in the principle of equifinality, therapists do not believe that the cause or etiology of a problem can be known. The fact that having been abused as a child or having an alcoholic parent may correlate with specific symptoms does not translate into "causes" of the current problem. One of the first lessons in a statistics class is that correlation does not equal cause. History taking may be a part of the therapy process, but it is done for perspective and an understanding of the context of the presenting problem rather than as a search for etiology, which cannot be known with certainty. Further, the fact of solution to a symptom or problem as a function of "working through" does not necessarily validate the cause-effect connection, although one could be seduced by success to a belief in the truth or validity of this connection. No matter how you got here, here is where you are. Now, where do you want to go?

17. Therapists are more likely to work to solve the problems clients present rather than to translate problems into a theoretical framework that defines what the "real" problems are and therefore must be resolved in order to solve the presenting problems. Thus, while therapists could use any story from the received-view theories, the focus would be on helping clients solve the problems that they presented. This may involve a reframe of a problem, providing an opportunity.

18. Ecosystemic therapists do not get caught up in the issue of brief versus long-term therapy. This dichotomy is based on received-view issues that have become a part of the folklore of normal mental health practice. Therapy takes as long as it takes. A related dichotomy in normative mental health practice is that between situational versus deep-seated problems. Many such dichotomies are nonissues for ecosystemic therapists. As Wátzlawick et al. (1974) noted,

> All theories have limitations which follow logically from their premises.
>
> In the case of psychiatric theories, these limitations are more often than not attributed to human nature. For instance, within the psychoanalytic framework, symptom removal without the resolution of the underlying conflict responsible for the symptom must lead to symptom substitution. This is not because this complication lies in the nature of the human mind: it lies in the nature of the theory, i.e., in the conclusions that logically follow from its premises. The behavior therapists, on the other hand, base themselves on learning and extinction theories and therefore need not worry about the dreaded consequences of symptom removal. (p. 26)

    Many such issues are tied to specific theories that are touted as describing human nature. Ecosystemic therapists are aware that by believing in such issues, they participate in creating problems that only exist because they logically fit that particular theoretical orientation. Problems are problems only from the framework and values that define them as problems. This is a statement that applies to therapists as well as clients.

19. Ecosystemic therapists are aware that many of the problems people experience are invented (although described as discovered by professionals marketing their own theoretical agendas). The plethora of popular-press books and questionnaires that appear in popular-press magazines are based on issues that are issues only from a particular frame of reference, based on normative data about how people are supposed to be. Thus, many of the problems that clients present for solution are the problems that we professionals create in order to solve

other problems. The issue here is whether we are making people aware of problems that they already had or whether we give people problems that may be worse than the problems the solutions would solve. The ecosystemic stance is that one does not discover problems. One invents them. Table 10.1

For ecosystemic therapists, a hierarchy of increasing organizational complexity might be described by table 10.1. Therapists are aware that the unit presenting itself for therapy is a part of a larger context. While a problem may be solved at the level of person, two-person, or family units, sometimes therapists may be called on to work with larger social contexts: that is, the community; the subculture; and at the political level, the society-nation. The implications of second-order cybernetics for mental health therapists described here are applicable to the individual, the couple, and the family. The choice of treatment unit is arbitrary, for we can cut up the world into as many subunits as we choose and develop what Gregory Bateson (1972) called an "ecology of ideas." When we operate from an ecosystemic perspective, we think relationally regardless of the size of the client system. Further, it is important to remember that the distinctions we make between things are not distinctions between the real things "out there." We must remember that our ecology of ideas are our inventions based on our invented distinctions and that to reify them as really existing out there is inappropriate. As Watts (1972) noted, "[T]his is no more than a way of thinking about the world: it is never actually divided" (p. 54). While Watts was making the point that our conceptual divisions of "out there" never fully correspond to the real "out there," second-order cybernetics (as well as quantum physics) makes us aware that the distinctions we make, the labels we apply, and the way we conceptualize and think about things create a reality that corresponds to our beliefs. Indeed, believing is seeing, and seeing is creating. We must therefore ask ourselves, "What other kind of world can we believe, see, and thus

Table 10.1 Components or Subsystems for an Undivided Universe

Components of the Universe	Components of the Individual
Cosmos	Individual
Earth	Organ Systems
Society-nation	Tissues
Culture-subculture	Cells
Community	Molecules
Family	
Two-person	
Person	

create?" The awareness that the world in which we experience ourselves is a story and that many stories about ourselves and the world are possible provides us with hope, tolerance, responsibility, uncertainty, and total freedom (Wátzlawick, 1984).[1]

---

[1] Chapter 10 is adapted from Becvar R., & Becvar, D. (1994), "The ecosystemic story: A story about stories," *Journal of Mental Health Counseling, 16*(1), 22–32. Copyright 1994 by American Mental Health Counselors Association. Adapted with permission.

Chapter 11

Reflections on Values in Systems Theory and Social Constructionism

The basic theme of this book is that well-intentioned efforts by therapists and educators using the normative, medical model may be contributing to what we view as a pandemic of mental illness. While the normative, medical model may be useful for treating problems in living described as disorders, an unanticipated consequence is that the model may create problems by attempting to solve problems. We suggested that second-order cybernetics and social constructionism may be antidotes to the pandemic. In fairness, we acknowledge that systems theory (second-order cybernetics) and social constructionism have also been criticized for not addressing important issues in our society. In this chapter, we address the critique of second-order cybernetics and social constructionism and suggest that the critics' observations are correct but that the limitations of the models may be one of their strengths.

A colleague asked,

> Given the ability of systems theory ideas to help us understand human behavior in more expansive ways, does system theory support any *action* based on these notions? A criticism has been leveled at social constructionist theory that it "takes no stands on anything"—it is just a way of thinking. Could the same be said of systems theory? It does not have any action component, so how can systems theory help us with responding to issues of social and racial injustice? Are there paths that systems theory can speak to address injustices in the world?

Our response to these questions addresses some basic issues that we believe practicing therapists should consider and issues that are important in the education of therapists—to help them develop an epistemology that has a conscious awareness of itself (G. Bateson, 1972; Keeney, 1983) to think and to think about their thinking. An awareness of one's epistemology seems to be essential in our work as therapists and in the education of therapists.

Our position is clear on one thing: Each theory is what it is and does what it does—no more and no less. It is an explanatory fiction. A theory should be judged on the basis of its consistency within itself and whether it is "useful" to help us understand our universe and to understand ourselves—attempting to understand ourselves. A theory should not be judged from a perspective and values from a different theory.

The critique of systems theory raised in the earlier questions is not valid at the level of first-order cybernetics. First-order cybernetics as it has evolved in the field of family therapy also has evolved a variety of models for the practice of family therapy. These models provide different avenues to solving the problems of individuals, couples, and families. As systemic models, the primary focus is on relationships and not individuals. However, while context and the interactional perspective is integral to the models, the observer or therapist is punctuated as an independent observer of the system (i.e., not a part of the system). In this sense, first-order cybernetics is thus inconsistent with its fundamental assumption: that everything in the universe is connected and interdependent. Observers are punctuated as independent of and cannot not influence the systems they observe. In other words, everything in the world is connected to every other thing and person—except the observer. There is an "out there" independent of the observer. Thus, one can observe without intruding on or influencing the system being observed.

Pragmatic first-order cybernetic theories for therapy reflect values and contain their own diagnostics of what is "normal," "functional," or "healthy" and what is not relative to these values. Thus, if therapy is successful from any of the models, then clients will be moving in the direction prescribed for "normal," "functional," or "healthy" as described by the theory. This may include promoting and valuing social justice. Indeed, clients typically use the language of the theory of the therapist as they describe their experiences. The following are among first-order cybernetic models in the field of family therapy:

- Bowen
- Object Relations
- Nagy
- Kempler
- Satir
- Minuchin

Most important for this discussion is that these first-order models describe dysfunctional and functional systems. Thus, each of these models espouses values, as do first-order therapies of normative, medical models in which the individual is the unit of analysis. Indeed, personality theories that form the conceptual basis for therapies focused on the individual diagnose disorder and order of "mental health." First-order therapy models are based on values and prescribe therapeutic outcomes based on values. These models also assume that one can observe without influencing that which is being observed—hence, objectivity.

Second- or higher-order cybernetics shares the systemic view of a totally conjoined universe. That is, there is but one system: the cosmos. Subsystems of this whole are punctuated as parts—but only in our conceptions or distinctions. Higher-order cybernetics is consistent with its basic assumption that all things and persons in the universe are connected and interdependent—including the observer. "Observers" are participant-observers in that which they observe. Moreover, this awareness includes observing their participation in the system being observed (which is a position from the "outside"—a dilemma that is unavoidable—it describes an infinity of observers observing observers participating in the system being observed). There is no outside of that to which we are necessarily a part. While no specific values are promoted at the level of higher-order cybernetics, this participant-observer perspective includes the awareness that observing in a system of which one is necessarily a member and whichever perturbation the observer as therapist uses reflects values. Indeed, not promoting a specific way of living based on selective values is a value. In essence it is impossible "intervene," which implies a position outside a system; perhaps *intravene* or *perturb* may better describe the relationship.

This distinction between first-order and second-order cybernetics is important in addressing the criticism that systems theory "takes no stand on anything." We view systems theory (second-order cybernetics) and social constructionism as metaperspectives. They are not pragmatic theories except in a broad sense. Systems theory as a model for therapy would focus on breaking existing patterns or relationships, and what evolves is that which evolves as the system seeks a different balance. It contains no prescription for a how a system is supposed to be. Social constructionism provides the metaview that we live our lives in stories of our cultures—or the stories live our lives for us. Any event can be storied in many ways—none of them "true" with a capital *T*.

As metatheories, both systems theory (second-order cybernetics) and social constructionism are rightly viewed as apolitical, amoral, and a-aesthetic. The questions critics of systems theory and social constructionism ask are political questions based on select values. Indeed, all categories punctuated by distinctions reflect values and politics. That is their utility, but some would say that is their weakness. By what standard based on what distinction do we judge strength and weakness, order and disorder, or good and bad? Both "take no stand on anything." We agree with this observation, but that "deficit" may be their utility and their value.

Again, systems theory has been rightfully judged as amoral, apolitical, and a-aesthetic. It is a metatheory and has no practical suggestions for its use in therapy. (Nature has no political or value objectives) It does not advocate for a specific world order. Systems theory is simply a map that provides us with a description (a social construction?) of relationships. Thus, in describing relationships of different levels of systems (rather like Russian dolls), it provides a conceptual map for an understanding of relationships between and within different levels of systems that we punctuate. It is important to remember that the universe or cosmos is one system and is not comprised of subsystems of the cosmos. We punctuate subsystems as we seek to know or have what we refer to as knowledge. Gregory Bateson (1972) and Flemons (1991) noted that the first act in the process of knowing is to punctuate a distinction. The distinctions we punctuate reflect values or purposes in punctuating a distinction. Punctuating distinctions create two entities (up and down, right and left, poor and rich, master and slave) that are really one entity because each is meaningless without the other. We forget that we create the distinctions in a world that is never actually divided (Watts, 1972). Thus, "categories" are constructed and named. These categories or distinctions are social constructions. Our story about these distinctions is a social construction. They choreograph a way of thinking about entities. The distinctions become a part of a society's worldview or Weltanschauung—which is a social construction containing the right ways to live in that society. They live in social and professional discourse. Indeed, professional categories and social constructions filter into social discourse.

We believe that values are implicit in social science research. Whatever knowledge or "facts" we find from our research is decontextualized—as though the entities we study are independent of context or based on a part or subsystem of a larger system. Further, research points to "facts" that reflect values; that is, what value is implicit in the research project; what are you walling in or walling out by the research question or hypothesis to be researched? In the German Nazi era, scientists were mandated to find research results that demonstrated the superiority of the Aryan "race." These "facts" often serve political and economic purposes. The master-slave relationship could be described as being justified because Black people (and people of other indigenous cultures) were dehumanized (i.e., were seen as inferior, less intelligent, less responsible, don't feel the pain that we do, etc.). In this same way, in a war, the enemy is dehumanized to justify killing them. Our society seeks "causes" of "mental" illness—a construct that focuses on the individual, out of context. The linear causal model lives in the worldview of our society.

Although "facts" are useful to justify the practices of certain relationships, a strong emotional assertion that plays to audiences' fears, jealousies, or bigotries can serve the same purpose as "facts." Politicians are masters at creating and maintaining social constructions that activate fear, anger, and righteousness. Of course, "facts" from one research project may contradict "facts" from a different research project. And the concept of "fact" is a social construction designed to give confidence in whatever it "validates." This necessarily depends on the research questions asked that reflect their political value. Like Charlie Brown once said, "I am giving you the right answers. You are asking the wrong questions." "Right" questions reflect the values implicit in research questions. The right or wrong questions are political and reflect values. A "fact" that some intervention based on a theory has worked with a client does not make it true. As philosopher of science, Helen Longino (1990) wrote, "Working is not an epistemological notion" (p. 9).

We view systems theories and all theories as social constructions—explanatory fictions. Almost all practical theories at the level of first-order cybernetics for the practice of individual and family therapy contain both diagnostics and prescriptions of desired future states. Their diagnostics and prescriptions fit the values of the culture in which the therapy is practiced. This is reflected in the accreditation and licensure requirements. The values of Western societies described in the introduction of this book, as well as in Chapter 1, are reflected in accreditation and licensure standards.

But systems theory did not find fertile ground in Western cultures because it challenged almost all the dominant Western values. It is important to remember that the values set forth here are social constructions implicit in the worldviews of Western societies. It is also important to remember that social constructionism is a social construct. Complicating this discussion is that the concepts of social and racial injustice are countercultural social constructions. These concepts challenge the values of Western societies referred to earlier. A true believer in the values of Western societies cannot comprehend the concept of racial and social injustices; "Yes, there are inequities, but it is their fault that they aren't getting their share."

To us a key question is whether a therapist in the process of doing therapy should promote racial and social justice in the process of therapy or in the discourse of the therapy. We believe a therapist cannot be apolitical, amoral, or a-aesthetic. All therapy is political. Indeed, even a theory that is apolitical, amoral, or unethical reflects values and is political in that the therapist would allow the system to seek its own level. We might infer that philosophically second-order cybernetics is akin to the worldview of the Tao Te Ching. What theory or metatheory do therapists use in their work? What values are implicit in their choice of theory or metatheory? Systems theory (second-order cybernetics) and social constructionism as metatheories may also be viewed as philosophies about theories of therapy by creating awareness that therapists promote values that are implicit in their pragmatic theories and are political.

A basic theme of this book is that almost all therapy is political, but it could be apolitical and freeing. Social constructionism and second-order cybernetics provide this perspective. However, we wonder, if therapists work to reduce racial or social injustice, then they are not violating their contract with the culture that licenses and sanctions their practice and socially prescribed role. We wonder also about how a therapist with Christian fundamentalist beliefs might work with a gay or lesbian couple or how a therapist with liberal beliefs might work with a couple with Chrisitan fundamentalist beliefs—or whether therapists should work with client systems that hold different values. Also, please note that financial reimbursements are dispensed only when diagnoses and treatments of individuals are consistent with the medical model and the worldview of our society. An important value of second-order cybernetics and social constructionism is to create this awareness that therapists promote select values and succumb to the political and cultural contexts that sanction their roles.

Second-order cybernetics and social constructionism are politically neutral—as are the pragmatic theories of Mental Research Institute (strategic) and behaviorism. To personify the concepts, both systems theory and social constructionism are indifferent to social arrangements and therapy outcomes. In this sense, they are like nature; that is, they do not prescribe or are not agonistic or vindictive or advocate selected arrangements and outcomes.

So, what does social constructionism provide? Simply said, social constructionism reminds us that we are living our lives in stories. This is an important contribution in that without this belief, we have no options. That is, if a story is not serving us well, then an alternate story may serve us better. Thus, the choice of story that we bring to any situation is relative to whether it serves the purposes. It reminds us that some people tend to have a story that says that our society should be socially and racially just. Others tell themselves the story that our society *is* socially and racially just, as prescribed by the values of Western society.

Systems theory can provide a description of the dynamics of relationships between individuals or between ideologies or different worldviews. It reminds us that we cannot do just one thing. There are no independent variables or entities in the universe. Moreover, the perspective of second-order cybernetics would have us be aware that we cannot not be a part of a system and aware of ourselves observing our participation in the system. Thus, we are always participating and observing our participation, which is also participation. There is no "outside of" for us. Our values as participants and observers of our participation are neutral regarding preferred outcomes. In a similar way, the observer is observing through some conceptual lens. This is a conscious awareness that both participation and observation cannot not affect the dynamics of the system—consistent with quantum physics. In effect, the apolitical stance of social constructionism and second-order cybernetics is a political stance.

The "neutrality" of systems theory and social constructionism are useful reminders that the responsibility for choice of values lies with the observer-participant and the coconstructor of stories. The responsibility rests with the therapists and their respect for the values of clients. What systems theory does well is to provide a language and map to describe relationships and provide an understanding of the dynamics involved in relationships—be it the relationship in the cosmos between orbiting planets and stars or the six relationships in a family of four as well as the relationship of each dyadic relationship to other relationships in the family and the relationship of each family member to other entities outside the family.

The focus of systems theory on relationship rather than the individual or entity is counter-Western-cultural. This difference reflects values. In essence, every entity stands in relationship with every other entity in the universe. No entity can exist or be understood in any way by itself. Identities are punctuated relative to an identity member. No entity can exist out of context—practically or conceptually. Thus, any ideology requires a competing or complementary ideology to be meaningful. Again, any distinction we punctuate creates a relationship without which each is meaningless without the other.

Unless a client's desired outcome is immoral, illegal, or unethical, we wonder if the therapist should have an investment in a specific outcome for therapy. And yet, we acknowledge that that the therapist cannot not value specific outcomes. In general terms, we believe the therapist should work for goals the clients desire, not what therapist diagnoses. That said, an exception might be that the process of therapy may plant seeds for a means to resolve future problems without a client's awareness. Another exception or contradiction to this is what Milton Erickson said in personal communication in 1979: "People come with problems they can't solve. I give them problems they can solve."

Therapists with a higher-order cybernetics perspective would see themselves as part of the system (client and therapist) and know their very presence constitutes an intervention and therefore self-consciously observe themselves being part of the system. Viewing themselves as independent observers of the client system (first-order cybernetics) is inconsistent with systems theory and the concept of a totally conjoined universe. They also view themselves as observers of themselves participating in the system. They also know that many different theories may be useful in the resolution of a client's problem. (Of course, single-theory therapists have a solution that fits all problems.)

Indeed, by asking questions, the therapist plants seeds and perhaps has begun to choreograph the therapeutic conversations that will follow. There are no value-neutral questions, observations, or stories in therapy. But are the questions we ask in the service of promoting the change the client wants from therapy? Again, what is the therapist walling in or walling out? There is no particular form that "psychotherapy" needs to take. Any technique judged ethical by the community is allowable. It can promote racial or social justice or support the status quo. An important question for therapists is, "Which form does my particular therapy take with which client system?" It cannot not take a form or promote a value by the therapist's participation and observation. (This may include ambiguous or neutral responses, which may be viewed as valuing clients' assuming responsibility and making value choices.) The choice of stories is relative—real events occur. Jews were killed. Hitler constructed a story that became a justification for this act. A story may be the basis for promoting what is called social justice and racial justice. How that event is storied is relative to the purposes the story would serve. The credo of race relationships for many years has been "separate but equal." Protestant and Catholic stories of Galileo's trial are very different and designed to promote select values and social and political purposes.

Should therapists have a value agenda? Keeney (1983) wrote, "It is impossible not to have an epistemology. Bateson (1977) elaborates this point: 'You cannot claim to have no epistemology. Those who so claim have nothing but a bad epistemology'" (p. 13). In this book we sought to help therapists, clients, and all people develop an epistemology that has a conscious awareness of itself in the process of helping them live more satisfying lives. Should therapists intervene directly or indirectly to make any client aware of a contradiction that Watts (1972) describes, "Yet the very society from which the individual is inseparable is using its whole irresistible force to persuade the individual that he is indeed separate! Society as we now know it is therefore playing a game with self-contradictory rules" (p. 64)? Should therapists participate with clients to "externalize" a diagnosis that has been "internalized" and has become part of clients' identities? Maybe the clients' relationships with their diagnoses helps them get a measure of freedom in relationships in which they are controlled.

Systems theory (second-order cybernetics) and social constructionism as metatheories do not prescribe any specific outcomes for therapy or societies. They remind us that desired outcomes or resolution of problems reflect the first-order theories of therapists, which become the lens through which client systems view their problems in living. By not promoting specific values, they remind us that we have choices in the degree to which we are informed of or know of options. By not promoting specific values, they give us no choice except to be free and to choose. Systems theory and social constructionism provide us with a measure of freedom from reified concepts in Weltanschauungs or worldviews.

Complementing these statements is an article written many years ago, "Therapy Is the Handmaiden of the Status Quo" (Halleck, 1971). And the status quo of our society has been punctuated by some as socially and racially unjust: "The world outside the self is indifferent to the fate of the self. . . . The world is indifferent toward humanity—it is not antagonistic" (Lopez, 2019, p. 484). Should that be an issue addressed by therapists directly or indirectly?

Chapter 12

A Story about Systemic and Social Constructionist Therapy

In this chapter, we present Dorothy's philosophy and process of therapy, which normalize and promote growth and wholeness. These even dare suggest that a spiritual dimension might be an appropriate focus for therapy. The philosophy and processes described may be an antidote to normative, medical-model therapies. The concepts could be applied to therapy with individuals, couples, or families.

A STORY OF THERAPY FOR CLIENTS

You have a story to tell, probably a problem-saturated story that has emerged, in part at least, as a function of prevailing beliefs in society about health and dysfunction. There are things in your life that you don't like, that you would like to see changed, and although you may not be saying so, you have at least an implicit idea about how you would like things to be. Not all your life is bad or unsuccessful, although that is what you may tend to focus on, at least as we begin our conversation together. The things that you describe as problematic are logical to context and thus, in some way that you probably don't understand, make sense.

You are not a diagnostic category, in spite of the fact that in order for you to get reimbursed by your insurance company, you may need me to provide a diagnosis.

Your needs and desires, your stories, are unique, and the therapy process is designed to fit you and your uniqueness.

I have many stories in my head that provide explanations and guidelines about individual, family, and systems behavior and the process of change, but I am not an expert.

My most important role is to listen to you, my client, as you tell your story; to recognize your expertise; to help you articulate possible solutions in the form of desired goals; and to search for instances in the past when you have been successful.

When I offer reflections and ideas, I will do so in a tentative and respectful manner that acknowledges my awareness that I don't have access to the Truth. Rather, I have knowledge that I can draw on that may be useful to you.

Together we will have a conversation in which we mutually influence one another in the process of cocreating a context that is logical to and supportive of the solutions or goals you desire.

It would be inconsistent for me to diagnose you for using, for example, the categories of the *DSM*. That is, I do not believe in diagnostic labels, which may participate in the further creation of a problem-saturated story that may become your reality.

I will explain my position to you, and together we will consider the ramifications of selecting a diagnosis and which diagnosis it might be if that is your choice. I will ask you to decide how to proceed regarding this issue.

I will respond to you as a unique system to the best of my ability. Where my ability to be effective is compromised by the limits of a third-party payer, I will let you know, and we will discuss this issue together.

The following statements reflect Dorothy Becvar's fundamental orientation to her work as a therapist (a story of therapy for therapists).

In addition to the theoretical perspective described here, given my spiritual, soul-healing orientation, the following thoughts and considerations also inevitably influence and guide my conversation with you:

- I assume that you and I are part of an interconnected whole and that not only do we mutually influence each other at a physical level, but we also have access to a level of communication and connectedness that exists at a soul level.
- I see all of us as aspects of a larger, divine universe, and I honor that perception relative to both to you and to me. I therefore truly love myself, thus having more to give to you, and I honor our encounter as a holy one.
- I acknowledge the sacred trust that you bestow on me when you come to me for professional help, and I will do everything in my power to be worthy of that trust by being respectful of you and by working in a moral and ethical manner.
- I will attempt to tune in to you, to hear you with both my ears and my intuition. You need to know that I trust the information I receive at a gut level, and I may present it to you as this seems appropriate.

- I may share my stories with you and/or describe my journey as a means of letting you know that we are all in this together, headed in the same general direction, even though we may be taking different paths.
- I believe that relationships may be understood as having a spiritual basis and connection, and I share my view that there are no accidents. I may try to provide you with such an awareness in the hope that it will enable you to understand your relationships in a more meaningful manner that facilitates your learning and growth.
- I will inquire about the role that religion and/or spirituality plays in your life, but I will take my cues from you about how best to proceed in this area.
- I do not make judgments about your behavior or that of others in your world. I assume that all behavior is logical in context, and I will help you to understand the way in which the behaviors you do not like somehow make sense. We will work together to achieve your goals relative to the behaviors that you find problematic.
- I will attempt to help you suspend judgment of other people and events as a way of shifting to a focus on solutions and the achievement of your desired goals.
- I accept you where you are, and I hope to facilitate your acceptance of others in your world in a similar manner.
- I assume that you and the others in your world are doing the best you and they can, given your particular circumstances.
- I will work to help you achieve your goals, but I also will recognize the limits of what may be possible. I acknowledge the appropriateness of the outcome, whatever that may look like.
- I will attempt to keep our focus on the here and now. I may ask about the past in order to get a better understanding of your context. I also may ask about your desired future state. However, I am aware that all we really have to work with is the present moment and that it is only by changing in the here and now that past and future events and their interpretations may be influenced.
- Given my trust in the universe, I look for the magical, synchronistic events in my life and world. I probably will point them out to you when it appears that you, too, may have experienced them.
- I may ask you about your dreams, and if you are interested, we may spend some time exploring them together. As we do so, however, I will encourage you to reach your own conclusions about their possible meanings and messages.
- I may encourage you to explore in some areas that are new for you relative to consciousness and the accessing of information: for example, through meditation or even by means of oracles or shamanic practices. At the same

time, I will encourage you to keep your feet planted firmly on the ground and to maintain, wherever possible, a sense of humor.

- I also may encourage you to explore various sources of the random or new information through reading and other activities in the effort to help you facilitate the creation of new, more useful realities.

- I may frame questions and offer reflections that encourage you to understand problems and crises as opportunities for growth and learning. We may even consider the possibility that they represent healing moments that are appropriate for you at a soul level.

- I may suggest that as we focus on solutions, we attempt to cocreate realities that enable you to become the person you would like to be and to achieve the kind of relationships you desire.

- I am aware that my belief in your ability to achieve your desired goals will have an influence on the outcome of our work together. I therefore will make every effort to support you, to validate you, to accept you, and to affirm my belief in your potential to succeed. At the same time, I will be realistic about what does not appear to be possible.

- I also am aware that your belief in your ability to achieve your desired goals will have an influence on the outcome of our work together. I will remind you of the influence of your beliefs on the creation of your reality.

- I am grateful for my view of life as a spiritual journey that may be undertaken as a path with heart, and I may speak to you about its importance for me in terms of obtaining a sense of meaning and purpose.

- I may encourage you to consider your heart's dream and the possibility of pursuing this dream, even if in only very small ways, if this seems appropriate or of interest to you.

- I will help you discern and choose a path with heart that seems right for you if that is your desire. I also will explain and help you find ways to avoid possible stumbling blocks, and I will support you in the best way I know how.

- I do not fear death or conversations about death, and I will be happy to talk with you about your thoughts and fears related to this topic. I also will invite you to experience the way in which life may be enriched as we come to terms with our own mortality and that of others.

- If our conversation includes religion or spirituality, I may talk to you about the challenge of living at two levels, and we may have conversations about how to integrate the spiritual and material aspects of our lives. While I probably won't have any definitive answers, we certainly may come up with some interesting questions.

- I will attempt to send you positive energy in the form of love.

With me, as I am with you in a manner consistent with these assumptions, my hope is that your experience of the counseling and therapy process will include the following:

- You will have a sense of connectedness and will feel accepted, validated, respected, and supported.
- You will feel not only that you have been heard but also that you have your own expertise as well as some other resources that you did not previously know were available to you.
- You will have a clearer idea about what it is you would like as well as a sense of what is possible, and you will feel hopeful about the attainment of your goals.
- You will have a new understanding of the degree to which you may influence the creation of your reality and will have new information about or perspectives on how to proceed.
- You will feel that healing at a very deep level is being facilitated and that your growth and development, or the unfolding of your vast potential, are being encouraged.
- You will experience the power of love and feel energized and renewed.

FRAMING QUESTIONS FOR CLIENT REFLECTION

- In what way does this situation or could this situation add meaning to your life?
- I wonder how we might look at and understand this situation differently.
- What opportunity for learning does this situation provide for you?
- I wonder whether there are themes or patterns that link this situation to others in your life.
- How do you think this situation might facilitate your growth?
- Suppose you had chosen this situation, knowing that it would be useful for you. I wonder what the usefulness of it might be.
- What resources do you possess that might be stimulated by this situation?
- I wonder about the timing of this situation and how it may be significant for you.
- How might you use this situation to benefit yourself and/or others in your world?
- I wonder in what direction this situation might be helping to point you.
- How could you use your creative energies to make something useful out of this situation?

- I wonder if the choices you are making reflect what you truly value.
- If you were to view this situation as representing the middle of an important aspect of your life story, whose outcome you knew was going to be positive, then how might this story end?
- I wonder, if this situation could talk, what it might be trying to tell you.
- If you thought of this situation as a map given to you by your higher power, then where do you think you might look for the buried treasure?
- I wonder whether your soul might be trying to communicate something to you through this situation.

Afterword

Writing and compiling the chapters in this book has been a challenging experience. We dared to challenge some sacred concepts that are deeply entrenched in the mental health field. Whether you agree with our concerns and/or our suggested alternatives or not, we appreciate your taking the time to read, consider, accept, or reject. We close with a summary of our story.

Therapists are consciously aware of all the traditional normative, medical-model constructs but do not use them in approaches to therapy that we suggest. Thus, ADHD, bipolar, prolonged grief, borderline, and other constructs are not part of the language system they use in therapy. Clients may use these constructs in their self-diagnosis, having gotten them from professional discourse that has flowed into social discourse. These would be explored in depth. By exploring the constructs in depth, a process of deconstruction or reconstruction is activated. A reframe may result that may "dis-solve" the problem or transform the problem into a different problem or an asset. Milton Erickson noted in personal communication in 1979 that people come with problems they can't solve. He gives them problems they can solve. A problem is punctuated as such by certain values.

Again, there are no problems floating around in space. They evolve by participation in societies that set standards for living that people use to compare themselves and others. In effect, people become "big brothers" watching themselves and watching others for deviations from standards. We believe problems evolve—not are caused—by sincere attempts to live life in accordance with the values in the worldviews of their societies. However, these standards are contradictory, paradoxical, utopian, and ever changing. Relationships with others are fraught with such difficulties, from which compliance or deviation from standards for living with each other are being judged.

Sincere attempts to adapt to the society and live by rules that are crazy making are very successful in producing the experience of craziness in individuals and relationships. However, to assign responsibility for not living successfully in such a society to the individual is in itself crazy making. Indeed, each relationship is its own miniature society with standards unique to that relationship. Attempts to enforce these standards on one another can be crazy making for each person and for the relationship. Going crazy may be one of many coping mechanisms when one feels powerless and has explored all logical options. Substance abuse may well be another coping mechanism. Therapy may be the court of last resort. But normative, medical models for therapy are extensions of the worldviews of societies that define problem behavior and use "treatment" methods that focus on the individual rather than the society that creates conditions for crazy making. Therapists thus become enforcing agents of their societies—along with social workers and police officers.

In this book we suggest an alternative model for a therapeutic process that

- normalizes problems in living and craziness;
- replaces or deconstructs metaphors that connote pathology;
- does not "treat" the construct (disorder—treating reifies the construct);
- views the client system in context and expands storytelling in therapy to include interpersonal contexts;
- explores how the problem, while unpleasant, may be useful in clients' lives may be solving other problems in clients' lives;
- explores the consequences, those punctuated as positive and negative, in clients' lives if the desired outcome from therapy is obtained (any desired outcome implies valuing the problems of the desired outcome rather than the problems in their current situation; there are no value- and problem-free solutions);
- slows down the process (the more serious the problem, the slower the pace of therapy should be);
- externalizes diagnostic constructs, objectifying them and locating them outside the client to facilitate conversations about them;
- views the problem as an opportunity for learning, growing, and transcendence;
- wonders about what is missing in clients' lives rather than what is wrong;
- wonders about what clients want to keep or conserve from their current lives as they move toward their preferred outcome; and
- facilitates clients wondering about their wondering and thinking about their thinking.

Ian Hacking (1995) wrote,

Inventing or molding a new kind, a new classification of people or of behavior may create new ways to be a person, new choices to make for good or evil. There are new descriptions, and hence new actions under a description. It is not that people change, substantively, but that as a point of logic new opportunities for action are open for them. (p. 289)

In closing, we hope that what we presented may be useful aesthetically and practically. But most of all, we hope that conversations may evolve that address the challenges that we perceive. Our attempted solutions consistent with the normative, medical model to the pandemic of mental illness may be the problem. More of the same or its opposite will not work. Indeed, what does *working* mean? That something "works" does not make it true: "Working is not an epistemological notion" (Longino, 1990, p. 93).

References

Bakewell, S. (2010). *How to live: Or, a life of Montaigne in one question and twenty attempts at an answer.* Other Press.

Barsky, A. J. (1988). The paradox of health. *New England Journal of Medicine, 318*(7), 414–418.

Bartlett, S. J. (1983). *Conceptual therapy: An introduction to framework-relative epistemology.* Crescere.

Bateson, G. (1972). *Steps to an ecology of mind.* Ballantine Books.

Bateson, G. (1979). *Mind and nature: A necessary unity.* Dutton.

Bateson, M. C. (2001, May 26–28). *Cybernetics of praxis and the praxis of cybernetics* [Conference brochure]. American Society for Cybernetics Conference, Vancouver, BC, Canada.

Becker, H. S. (1967). Whose side are we on? In W. J. Filstead (Ed.), *Qualitative methodology: Firsthand involvement with the social world* (pp. 239–247). Markham.

Becvar, D. (1983). *The relationship between the family and society in the context of American ideology: A systems theoretical perspective* [Unpublished doctoral dissertation]. St. Louis University.

Becvar, D. S., & Becvar, R. J. (2013). *Family therapy: A systemic integration* (8th ed.). Pearson Education.

Becvar, R. J., Becvar, D. S., & Bender, A. E. (1982). Let us first do no harm. *Journal of Marital and Family Therapy, 8*(4), 385–391.

Beer, S. (2004). What is cybernetics? *Kybernetes, 33*(3/4), 853–863.

Berkus, R. (1990). *In celebration of friendship.* Red Rose Press.

Boisvert, C. M., & Faust, D. (2002). Iatrogenic symptoms in psychotherapy: A theoretical exploration of the potential impact of labels, language and belief systems. *American Journal of Psychotherapy, 56*(2), 244–259.

Boscolo, L., Cecchin, G., Hoffman, L., & Penn, P. (1987). *Milan systemic family therapy: Conversations in theory and practice.* Basic Books.

BrainyQuote. (n.d.). *William Blake quotes.* Retrieved September 11, 2024, from https://www.brainyquote.com/quotes/william_blake_150110

Brand, S. (1974). *II cybernetic frontiers.* Random House.

Breunlin, D. C., & Jacobsen, E. (2014). Putting the "family" back into family therapy. *Family Process, 53*(3), 462–475. https://doi.org/10.1111/famp.12083

Briggs J. P., & Peat, F. D. (1984). *Looking glass universe: The emerging science of wholeness.* Simon & Schuster.

Bronowski, J. (1978). *The origins of knowledge and imagination.* Yale University Press.

Caplan, N., & Nelson, S. D. (1973). On being useful: The nature and consequences of psychological research on social problems. *American Psychologist, 28*(3), 199–211.

Capra, F. (1983). *The turning point: Science, society, and the rising culture.* Bantam Books.

Churchman, C. W. (1979). *The systems approach and its enemies.* Basic Books.

Dell, P. (1983). From pathology to ethics. *Family Therapy Networker, 1*(6), 29–64.

Erickson, M. (1979). Personal Communication.

Flemons, D. G. (1991). *Completing distinctions.* Shambala.

Foulkes, L., & Andrews, J. L. (2023). Are mental health awareness efforts contributing to the rise in reported mental health problems? A call to test the prevalence inflation hypothesis. *New Ideas in Psychology, 69*, 1–6.

Fox, D. M. (1990). Health policy and the politics of research in the United States. *Journal of Health Politics, Policy and Law, 15*(3), 481–499.

Gadamer, H.-G. (1996). *The enigma of health: The art of healing in a scientific age* (J. Gaiger & N. Walker, Trans.). Stanford University Press.

Gale, J. (1992). *A field guide to qualitative inquiry and its clinical relevance* [Unpublished manuscript].

Gergen, K. J. (1991). *The saturated self: Dilemmas of identity in contemporary life.* Basic Books.

Hacking, I. (1995). *Rewriting the soul: Multiple personality and the sciences of memory.* Princeton University Press.

Hacking, I. (1999). *The social construction of what?* Harvard University Press.

Haley, J. (1976). *Problem-solving therapy: New strategies for effective family therapy.* Jossey-Bass.

Halleck, S. (1971). Therapy is the handmaiden of the status quo. *Psychology Today, 4*, 30–34.

Hoffman, L. (1990). A constructivist position for family therapy. In B. P. Keeney, B. F. Nolan, & W. L. Madsen (Eds.), *The systemic therapist* (Vol. 1, pp. 3–31). Systemic Therapy Press.

Howard, G. S. (1991). Culture tales: A narrative approach to thinking, cross-cultural psychology, and psychotherapy. *American Psychologist, 46*(3), 187–197.

Hoyt, M. F., & Gurman, A. S. (2012). Wither couple/family therapy? *Family Journal, 20*(1), 12–17.

Jackson, D. D. (2009). The myth of normality. In W. A. Ray (Ed.), *Don. D. Jackson: Interactional theory in the practice of therapy: Selected papers* (Vol. 2, pp. 217–233). Zeig, Tucker & Theisen.

Kaptchuk, T. J. (2023, October 10). No better than a placebo. *The New York Times.* https://www.nytimes.com/2023/10/10/opinion/decongestant-placebo-medicine.html

Keeney, B. P. (1983). *Aesthetics of change*. Guilford Press.

Klein, A. C. (2016). Revisiting ritual. *Tricycle: The Buddhist Review, 26*(1), 68–73.

Kuhn, T. S. (1970). *The structure of scientific revolutions* (2nd ed.). University of Chicago Press.

Lather, P. (1986). Research as praxis. *Harvard Educational Review, 56*(3), 257–277.

Longino, H. E. (1990). *Science as social knowledge: Values and objectivity in scientific inquiry*. Princeton University Press.

Lopez, B. (2019). *Horizon*. Alfred A. Knopf.

Luhrmann, T. M. (2015, January 18). Redefining mental illness. *The New York Times*, 5.

Mair, M. (1988). Psychology as storytelling. *International Journal of Personal Construct Psychology, 1*(2), 125–139.

Malcolm, J. (1978, May 15). A reporter at large: The one-way mirror. *New Yorker*, 39–114.

Maturana, H. R. (1975). The organization of the living: A theory of the living organization. *International Journal of Man-Machine Studies, 7*(3), 313–332.

Mindfulness 360. (2017, February 20). *"A Chinese farmer story"—Alan Watts* [Video]. YouTube. https://www.youtube.com/watch?v=sWd6fNVZ20o

Minuchin, S. (1984). *Family kaleidoscope*. Harvard University Press.

Morris, J. (2017). What's become of family therapy. *Family Therapy Magazine, 16*(4), 9–11.

Næss, A., with Haukeland, P. I. (2002). *Life's philosophy: Reason and feeling in a deeper world* (R. Huntford, Trans.). University of Georgia Press.

National Institute of Mental Health. (2023, March). *Mental illness*. https://www.nimh.nih.gov/health/statistics/mental-illness#part_2555

Oyle, I., & Jean, S. (1992). *The wizdom within: On daydreams, realities, and revelations*. H. J. Kramer.

Pearce, J. C. (1988). *The crack in the cosmic egg: Challenging constructs of mind and reality*. Julian Press.

Plas, J. M. (1986). *Systems psychology in the schools*. Pergamon Press.

Rainwater, L. (1967). The revolt of the dirty-workers. *Trans-action, 5*(2).

Ray, W. A. (2005). On being cybernetic. *Kybernetes, 34*(3/4), 360–364.

Ricoeur, P. (1978). The problem of the foundation of moral philosophy. *Philosophy Today, 22*(3), 175–192.

Roach, K. (2017, December 25). Diagnosing mental illness. *St. Louis Post Dispatch*, 4.

Sarason, S. B. (1972). *The creation of settings and the future societies*. Jossey-Bass.

Sarason, S. B. (1981). *Psychology misdirected*. Free Press.

Satir, V. (1967). *Conjoint family therapy: A guide to theory and technique* (Rev. ed). Science and Behavior Books.

Saxby, D. (2023, November 18). This is not the way to help depressed teenagers. *The New York Times*. https://www.nytimes.com/2023/11/18/opinion/teenagers-mental-health-treatment.html

Schofield, W. (1986). *Psychotherapy: The purchase of friendship*. Transaction Books.

Segal, L. (1986). *The dream of reality: Heinz von Foerster's constructivism*. Springer.

Shields, C. G., Wynne, L. C., McDaniel, S. H., & Gawinski, B. A. (1994). The marginalization of family therapy: A historical and continuing problem. *Journal of Marital and Family Therapy, 20*(2), 117–138.

Stromberg, J. (2012, July 23). What is the nocebo effect? *Smithsonian Magazine*. https://www.smithsonianmag.com/science-nature/what-is-the-nocebo-effect-5451823/

Szasz, T. S. (1970). *Ideology and insanity: Essays on the psychiatric dehumanization of man*. Doubleday.

Thomas, L. (1979). *The medusa and the snail: More notes of a biology watcher*. Viking Press.

Varela, F. J. (1979). *Principles of biological autonomy*. Elsevier North Holland.

von Foerster, H. (1981). *Observing systems*. Intersystems.

Watts, A. (1972). *The book: On the taboo against knowing who you are*. Vintage Books.

Watts, A. (Writer), & Moore, R. (Director). (1959, December 31). Eastern wisdom and modern life. [TV series episode]. In R. Peyton (Producer), *Eastern Wisdom and Modern Life*. KQED.

Wátzlawick, P. (Ed.). (1984). *The invented reality: How do we know what we believe we know?* Norton.

Wátzlawick, P., Weakland, J. H., & Fisch, R. (1974). *Change: Principles of problem formation and problem resolution*. Norton.

White, M., & Epston, D. (1990). *Narrative means to therapeutic ends*. W. W. Norton.

Wilson, R. A. (1986). *The new inquisition: Irrational rationalism and the citadel of science*. Falcon Press.

Wilson, R. A. (1990). *Quantum psychology: How brain software programs you and your world*. New Falcon.

Wolfe, C. (1998). *Critical environments: Postmodern theory and the pragmatics of the outside*. University of Minnesota Press.

Wright, L. M., & Leahy, M. (1994). Calgary family intervention model: One way to think about change. *Journal of Marital and Family Therapy, 20*(4), 381–395.

Yalom, I. D. (2015). *Creatures of a day: And other tales of psychotherapy*. Basic Books.

Index

adolescents, xvii, 57
"adult child of a dysfunctional family"
(diagnosis), 45
Andrews, J. L., xvi–xvii
animals, 29; neuroses induced in, 42;
relationship with domesticated,
58–59
Aristotelian logic, 16

bad things: clinical bias on, 43–44, 58;
good thing causes weighed equally
with, 45–46
Barsky, A. J., 17, 18, 38–39
Bartlett, S. J., xv, 16–17
Bateson, Gregory, 29, 42, 68, 101; on
awareness of epistemologies, 74; on
clinical bias, 43, 58; conversation
with daughter, xviii–xix; on creating
distinctions, 25, 32, 98; on ecology
of ideas, 93; on mind in nature, 86;
on pathologies of epistemology, 21;
on universal mind, 15
Bateson, Mary Catherine, xviii–xix
Becker, H. S., 30–31
Becvar, Dorothy, 37, 94, 103, 104
Becvar, Raphael, 37, 94
behavior: criteria for acceptable, 25–26,
33; hereditary components of, 24;
"scientizing," 40; self-defeating, xv,

5, 41; systems theory on maintenance
of, 78
Berkus, Rusty, 57
bias, clinical, 43–46, 58
Blake, William, 13
Bohr, Niels, 18–19
Boisvert, C. M., 40
Bowenian model, 64, 76, 88
Brand, Stewart, 42

Caplan, N., 77
cause, of problems: linear thinking and,
79, 98; outside of "normal" as, 70;
systems theory on, 79, 91, 109
childhood: dysfunction in, 44, 45;
impacts of idyllic, 35, 45; repressed
memories from, 45; worldview
creation in, 26–27
Chinese farmer (morality tale), 45–46
clients: cycle of increase in therapists
and, 37, 51, 56, 80–81; deferring
wisdom to therapists, 10; diagnostic
process explained to, 103, 104;
framing questions for, reflection,
107–8; identity informed by
diagnosis, 55–56, 78; individuality,
103; self-diagnosis, 24, 35, 50, 109;
story of therapy for, 103–7; therapist
providing stories for, 40, 41, 86;

therapy centered around, 11, 88; therapy goals explained to, 107. *See also* therapist-client relationship

clinical bias, 43–46, 58

collective consciousness, 25, 28, 35, 64

conceptual therapy, 6, 76

conjoined universe: awareness of, xviii; components or subsystems of, 93, *93*; systemic view of, 64–65, 97

conscious living, xviii, xix; context role in, 12; limits of, 3–12; socialization of stories and, 27–28

constructivism, 13; about, 63, 65, 68–71; as mysticism, 20–21; reality and, 65; scientific investigation and, 20, 65; as social construction, 68

context. *See* political, social, and cultural contexts

COVID-19 pandemic, xvi, 3

cultural context. *See* political, social, and cultural contexts

culture, society contrasted with, 30

cybernetics, 7; defining, 13; first-order, evolution of, 96; first-order, models, 64, 96–97; first-order compared with second-order, 33, 64–65, 67–68, 97; move from first-to-second order, 77; as mysticism, 20–21; nocebo effect and, 58; observation in, 64, 65, 67–68, 96, 100; reality and, 65; second-order, 23, 33–34, 51–52, 57, 64–65, 67–68, 70, 76–77, 79, 84, 85, 87–93, 95, 97–102; systems theory kinship with, 32, 33, 67–68; values in, 66–67, 96–97

deficit: language and terminology, 35, 40; model, 43; therapists advertising treatment of, 10; value of, 97

Dell, Paul, 7, 12, 70

depression, xvii, 6–7, 91

diagnosis: "adult child of a dysfunctional family," 45; client identity informed by, 55–56, 78; economic and political aspect of, 51, 83; genetics relation to, 54; impacts

of, 8–9, 38, 41, 51, 54, 78–79; marriage and, 55; of mental illness, 8–9, 10–11, 26, 35, 38, 49–50, 51, 80, 109; obstacles of formal, 78–79; responsibility absolved with, 55; reverse approach to, 51; self, 24, 35, 50, 109; standardization of problems and, 49–50, 55; therapist not providing, 87–88

Diagnostic and Statistical Manual of Mental Disorders (DSM), 8, 84; diagnosis creating identity for client, 78; increase in disorders in, xix, 69; licensing and, 75; social and cultural contexts missing in, 25, 75, 82; as social construction, 34, 82; therapists legal battle on, 74; therapists views on diagnoses from, 78–79; therapy reimbursement relation to, 83

diagnostic process: client informed about, 103, 104; ecosystemic model and, 87, 89; failings around, 10–11, 33–34, 54; "looping effect" in, 55; standard values applied in, 49

disease, 39, 54

disorders. *See* deficit; *Diagnostic and Statistical Manual of Mental Disorders*; dysfunction; mental illness

distinctions: creating, 25, 32, 98; meditation and, 48; relationships role in, 73; social values creating, 28–29; Taoist thought on, 31

divorce, 8, 9–10

domestication, 3, 29

DSM. See Diagnostic and Statistical Manual of Mental Disorders

dysfunction: in childhood, 44, 45; identification of group-based, 37–38; invention of, 41; language of, 35

ecology of ideas, 93

economics: of diagnosis, 51, 83; of health, 39; of normative medical therapy, 81; virtue relation to, 14

ecosystemic paradigm: about, 85–87; diagnostic process and, 87, 89; implications for therapists, 87–94; organizational complexity and, 93, *93*; paradox in, 90–91; stories about life experience and, 85–86
Eddington, 20
enlightenment, 47
epistemological therapy, xv
epistemologies: awareness of, 74; pathologies of, xvii–xviii, 21; as study of relationships, 20
equifinality, 79, 91
Erickson, Milton, 88, 89, 101, 109
"evidence-based" treatments, 75

fact and truth, 16, 87, 98, 111
family therapy. *See* marital and family therapy
Faust, D., 40
fears, health, 17–18, 39
feelings: feelings about, 6, 39–40, 91; political context of, 31
first-order change, xvii
Flemons, Douglas, 25, 98
Foulkes, L., xvi–xvii
Fox, D. M., 19
Freudian psychology, 66

Gadamer, H.-G., 44, 48, 49–50
genetics, 24, 54
Gergen, K. J., 26, 40
good things: bad things causes equally weighed with, 45–46; clinical bias on, 43, 44, 58
Gurman, A. S., 74

Hacking, Ian, 55, 110–11
Haley, Jay, 56, 76, 80
Halleck, S., 102
happiness. *See* unhappiness
Haukeland, P. I., 3, 4, 53
health: commercialization of, 39; decline in sense of personal, 38; fears about, 17–18, 39; illness discussions

prioritized over, 48–49; standard values promotion and impacts on, 48–50
Howard, G. S., 68
Hoyt, M. F., 74
hypochondria, 7, 17–18, 39, 40, 57

individuality: client, 103; diagnostic categories and treatment relation to, 25, 55; normalcy relation to, 11–12; normative medical therapy disregard for, xviii, 11, 12, 54; standardized treatment ignoring, 55; of stories about life experience, 28, 87, 93–94; of worldviews, 28
interconnectivity: components of, 93, *93*; therapeutic models and practice including, 81–82. *See also* collective consciousness; conjoined universe; systems theory

Jackson, Don, xx

Keeney, B. P., 52, 56, 101
knowledge and knowing, 68; distinctions creation and, 25, 32, 98; limits of, 13–21; relationships and, 73; worldview relation to, 26
Kuhn, T. S., 14, 87

licensing, 30–31, 32, 41, 67, 75, 82, 83–84
linear thinking, 44, 79, 98
Longino, Helen, 18, 98
Luhrmann, T. M., 78

Mair, M., 27, 68
marital and family therapy: first-order cybernetics models, 64; marginalization of, 74; quantum physics lessons and, 18–19; systems theory and, 13, 18, 73–84
marriage, 9–10, 55
the mask, formation of, 3–4
Maturana, H. R., 51–52

media, 25, 39
medical therapy, normative. *See*
    normative medical therapy
meditation, 48, 105–6
Mental Health Awareness Month, 55
mental illness: brain chemistry focus
    with, 54; categories and language
    of, xix, 8, 9, 26, 38, 56; COVID-19
    pandemic and, 3; definitions of, 8–9,
    26, 33, 38, 56, 80–81; diagnostic
    process for, 10–11; as disease, 54;
    Googling symptoms of, 55; invention
    of, 41; liberal definition of, 8–9,
    80–81; Mental Health Awareness
    Month and, 55; normalcy deviation
    seen as, 48; normalizing, xix–xx,
    12; pandemic of, xvi, xvii, 6, 53, 95;
    percentage of people worried about,
    57; rise in, xvi–xvii; Schofield on
    definitions/diagnoses of, 8–9, 26, 38,
    51, 80; self-consciousness relation
    to beliefs about, 4, 8, 47, 50, 56–57;
    self-diagnosis of, 35, 50, 109; as
    social construct, 5, 98; social context
    of, 54, 82; solutions for escalation
    of, 35; standardization of problems
    in diagnosis of, 49–50; symptoms
    relation to survival in relationships,
    56, 76; systems theory view of,
    33–34, 53–54, 63; wild animal
    domestication and, 29
mind, 86; quantum physics on, 15;
    worldview creation in, 26–27
Minuchin, Salvador, 41, 64, 73, 76, 93
Morris, J., 74

Næss, Arne, 3, 4, 53
Nagy, 64, 76
nature, 31, 35, 86
Nelson, S. D., 77
neuroses, inducing, 42
Newtonian physics, xvii, 14, 65, 67, 79
nocebo effect, 58
normalcy, xix–xx; assessment relation
    to, 64; cultural stories of, 52;

definitions of, 33; of depression, 6–7;
    deviations from, as mental illness,
    48; divorce and concepts of, 9–10; as
    exception, 11; first-order cybernetic
    theories on, 96; individuality relation
    to, 11–12; "life happens" concept
    and, 7; others role in feelings of, 57;
    problems defined in relation to, 70;
    as "right" way, 34; systems-oriented
    therapist and disorder, 34; therapists
    education and assessment around, 16,
    89; therapy seen as path to, 35, 55
normative medical therapy: alternative
    philosophy and process to,
    103–8, 110; assessment in, 64;
    characteristics of, 63; clinical bias
    in, 43–45; economic rewards for,
    81; educating oneself about, 82;
    individuality disregard in, xviii, 11,
    12, 54; mental illness pandemic
    and, 95; nocebo effect and, 58;
    observation in, 64; pathologies
    of epistemology in, xvii–xviii;
    situational compared with deep-
    seated problems in, 92; systems-
    oriented therapy contrasted with, 34,
    69–70; therapist educating oneself
    on, 82

observation: in conjoined universe, 64–
    65, 97; in cybernetics, 64, 65, 67–68,
    96, 100; Newtonian physics and, 67;
    object changed by, 42, 64–65, 67–68;
    objectivity and, 20, 64; outside of
    system, 33, 100; quantum physics
    and, xvii, 64–65; of social rituals,
    4; societal values reflected in, 32;
    systems theory on, 14, 32, 33, 77,
    100; in therapy, 57, 64; tools, 65

pandemic: COVID-19, xvi, 3; of mental
    illness, xvi, xvii, 6, 53, 95
"The Paradox of Health" (Barsky),
    38–39
pathologies of epistemology, xvii–xviii,
    21

Pearce, J. C., 26
personality inventory, 65
physics. *See* quantum physics
placebo effect, 58
Plas, J. M., 86
political, social, and cultural contexts:
DSM disregard of, 25, 75, 82;
identity relation to, 100; of mental
illness, 54, 82; of problems, 15,
25–26, 31, 54, 70; research in, 19;
self as separate from, 80; social
constructions in, 98; systems theory
neutrality around, 100; therapists
awareness of, 99; of therapy, 31;
worldview and, 27
prevalence inflation hypothesis, xvi–xvii
problems: animals in wild and, 29;
assumptions about origins of, 24–25;
change across time, 69; classification
of, 18; escalating, 5; feelings about
feelings as, 6, 39–40, 91; as invented,
41, 92–93; linear thinking about, 44,
79; multiple theories for solutions
to, 101; offering solvable, 101, 109;
outside of "normal" as cause of, 70;
as part of life, 12, 40, 53; political
and social context of, 15, 25–26, 31,
54, 70; questions asked about, 5, 41,
75–76, 98, 107–8; relationships and
evolution of, 24, 29; relationships
impacted by solutions to, 48, 80;
situational compared with deep-
seated, 92; solutions creating
other, 47–48, 53, 56, 90, 111;
standardization of, 49–50, 55; stories
about life experience relation to, 24–
25, 41–42; systems theory on, 14–15,
16; therapist choice of words about,
89; therapists advertising, treated, 10,
34–35; in therapy, beginnings and
endings and, 23; treating values over,
7, 12, 50. *See also* bad things

quantum physics, 18–19; on nonlocal
universal mind, 15; observation and,
xvii, 64–65; uncertainty principle in,
76–77
questions: about problems, 5, 41, 75–76,
98, 107–8; reflection, for clients,
107–8; about stories, 41, 107–8

reality: cybernetics and constructivism
on, 65; normative medical model on,
63; social construction of, 51–52, 65,
66; stories about life experience as,
69, 86; worldview as, 87
regulation. *See* sanctions and regulations
relationships: adolescent, 57; with
animals, 58–59; epistemology as
study of, 20; evolution of problems
and, 24, 29; knowing and, 73;
problems arising within, 24, 29; role
in distinctions, 73; self-consciousness
and, 4; sense of self based on, 71;
solutions to problems impact on,
48, 80; stories about life experience
defining, 86, 91; survival in, 56, 76,
110; systems theory and, xx, 70,
77–78, 91, 97–98, 100; worldview
creation relation to, 26–27. *See also*
therapist-client relationship
responsibility, 55, 63
Ricoeur, P., 85, 86
Roach, K., 78–79

sanctions and regulations: diagnoses
and, 33; economic rewards by
staying within, 81; therapist role
relation to, 8, 30–31, 32, 41, 49, 67,
81
Sarason, Seymour, 27, 32, 67
Satir, Virginia, 6, 39, 64, 76, 91
Schofield, William: on definitions of
mental illness, 8–9, 26, 38, 51, 80;
on diagnosis impacts, 8–9, 38, 41;
on prevention of unhappiness, 6; on
therapist and client increase cycle,
37, 51, 56; on utopian notions, 70
science: constructivism and, 20, 65;
contributions from social, 37–42;
recursive system-maintaining

practice around, 19; systems theory and, 32, 76, 77; theories, usefulness of, 96

self-consciousness, 65; mask formation and, 3; mental illness beliefs relation to, 4, 8, 47, 50, 56–57; paradox of, 4–5, 47; relationships and, 4; societal importance of, 3

self-defeating behaviors, xv, 5, 41

Shields, C. G., 74

slavery, 28

social constructionism, xx; about, 63, 65, 68–71, 97; assessment process and, 64, 69; constructivism and, 68; critiques of, 95, 97; reality notions relation to, 51–52, 65, 66; stories about life experience and, 68, 97, 100; values in, 95–102; worldviews and, 27, 28, 52

social context. *See* political, social, and cultural contexts

socialization, 4; conscious living and, of stories, 27–28; domestication kinship with, 3, 29; process, 26; quantum physics and, 10–11; worldviews and, 26, 27, 85

social paradigm, violations of, 26, 29–30

social rituals, 4

social science. *See* normative medical therapy; science; therapy

society: adaptation to, 110; culture contrasted with, 30; service to general good of, 13; socialization process and, 3–4; social rituals within, 4; therapists role in, 30–31, 32, 37, 67, 69, 99; therapists within not apart from, 8, 23, 32, 69, 75, 76, 80; treatment of violations, 29–30; values, 25, 28–29, 32, 99; Western, 75, 99; worldview creation from, 27, 30

solutions, to problems, 35; creating other problems, 47–48, 53, 56, 90, 111; multiple theories for,

101; relationships impacted by, 48, 80

soul: communication from, 108; healing, 104, 106; Watts on, 15, 80

Sound of Music (film), 23–24

standardization, 48–50, 55

Steps to an Ecology of Mind (Bateson, G.), 86

stories, about life experience: adolescent, 57; awareness, impacts of, 57; clinical bias and, 43; conscious living and socialization of, 27–28; "crazy making," 69; cultural scripts of, 52; ecosystemic paradigm and, 85–86; feelings created with, 39–40; judgment of, 68; meaning lies in, 7–8, 11; power of normalizing or pathologizing, 41; problems relation to, 24–25, 41–42; questions about, 41, 107–8; as reality, 69, 86; relationships defined by, 86, 91; as self-defeating, 41; social constructionism and, 68; therapist-client relationship and, 56, 79, 88; therapists providing client, 40, 41, 86; as traumatic, 81; unique, 28, 87, 93–94; worldview informed by, 27, 52, 68

substance abuse, 48, 110

symptoms, 76, 110; Googling, of mental illness, 55; systems theory view of, 79; as tactics, 56; theories about removal of, 92

systems theory: about, 13–14, 32–33, 63–71; as alternative therapy, 63; approach to therapy, 14, 69, 70–71, 73–84; on behavior maintenance, 78; on cause of problems, 79, 91, 109; client provided information about, 104–5; on conjoined universe, 64–65, 97; critiques of, 14, 76, 95, 96; double-consciousness for therapists using, 82–83; on fact and truth, 16, 87, 98, 111; on integrated self, 79–80; marital and family therapy and,

13, 18, 73–84; mental illness viewed from, 33–34, 53–54, 63; neutrality of, 100; normative medical-oriented therapy contrasted with, 34, 69–70; on observation, 14, 32, 33, 77, 100; relationships and, xx, 70, 77–78, 91, 97–98, 100; science and, 32, 76, 77; social science research and, 76; societal story and traditions relation to, 13–14, 68; therapists role in, 14, 23, 79, 81; thinking necessary in, 16; values in, 95–102; Western society and, 75, 99. *See also* cybernetics

Szasz, Thomas, xix, 6, 54

Taoist worldview, 31, 99
theories: as social constructions, 99; on symptoms removal, 92; usefulness of, 96. *See also* cybernetics; social constructionism; systems theory
therapist-client relationship: approach to, 87; as co-creators, 88; confrontation and, 89–90; guide for, 103–7; outcomes and, 101; resistance and, 89, 90; stories and, 56, 79, 88; systems theory on, 79
therapists: advertising problems treated, 10, 34–35; agenda of, 101–2; agenda or investment of, 91; clients deferring wisdom to, 10; contributions from, 37–42; cycle of increase of clients and, 37, 51, 56, 80–81; defining term, xxi; demand for, 56; diagnosis not provided by, 87–88; on *DSM*-based diagnoses, 78–79; *DSM* legal battle by, 74; ecosystemic paradigm implications for, 87–94; education and assessment of normalcy, 16, 89; focus on "part" over whole, 54; hierarchal role in society, 30–31; liberal definition of mental illness by, 8–9, 80–81; list of problems treated by, 34–35; marital and family therapy, 13, 18, 64, 73–84;

normalizing over pathologizing approach by, 12; societal role of, 8, 30–31, 32, 37, 41, 49, 67, 69, 81, 99; within society rather than apart, 8, 23, 32, 69, 75, 76, 80; systems-oriented contrasted with medical-oriented, 34, 69–70; systems theory on role of, 14, 23, 79, 81; theory choice relation to values of, 99; treating values over problems, 7, 12, 50. *See also specific topics*
therapy: alternative philosophy and process to normative, 103–8, 110; beginnings and endings in, 23–35; brief compared with long-term, 92; client-centered, 11, 88; conceptual, 6, 76; context disregarded in, 31; epistemological, xv; goals explained to client, 107; observation in, 57, 64; as opportunity for growth, xv; pathologies of epistemology in, xvii–xviii, 21; placebo effect in, 58; political context of, 31; reimbursement for, 55, 83, 99, 103; self-contradictory rules of, 101–2; status quo and, 102; systems theory approach to, 14, 69, 70–71, 73–84; systems theory viewed as alternative, 63; values-based, 66–67. *See also* marital and family therapy; normative medical therapy; *specific topics*
"Therapy Is the Handmaiden of the Status Quo" (Halleck), 102
thinking: linear, 44, 79, 98; as painful, 53; systems theory and, 16
Thomas, Lewis, 76–77
truth. *See* fact and truth

uncertainty principle, 76–77
unhappiness: avoidance of, 39, 70; as part of life, 6–7, 81; self-scrutiny relation to, 17–18; therapist skill in preventing, 56
uniqueness. *See* individuality

universe, undivided. *See* conjoined universe

values: collective consciousness and, 64; in cybernetics, 66–67, 96–97; diagnostic process and standard, 49; health impacted by imposing standardized, 48–50; living up to prescribed, 70; observation reflection of, 32; societal, 25, 28–29, 64, 99; in systems theory and social constructionism, 95–102; theory choice relation to, 99; therapist, 101; treating, over problems, 7, 12, 50; Western society, 99; worldviews relation to, 27, 28–29, 66–67
violations, of social paradigm, 26, 29–30
Von Foerster, Heinz, 77

Watts, Alan, 4–5, 101–2; Chinese farmer story of, 45–46; on conceptual divisions of "out there," 93; on insoluble problems, 41; on soul, 15, 80; systems theory and, 32, 80, 93;

on worldview and socialization, 26, 27, 85
Wátzlawick, P., xvii, 92
weltanschauung. *See* worldview
Western society, 75, 99
Whitaker, 64
Whitehead, Alfred North, 16, 20
Wilson, R. A., 14, 15, 27–28
work ethic, 14
worldview (weltanschauung): acceptance of differing, xviii, 12; attachment to, 87; creation of, 26–27; culture relation to, 30; distinctions role in, 98; problems assessed in relation to, 24; as reality, 87; social constructionism and, 27, 28, 52; socialization and, 26, 27, 85; society and creation of, 27, 30; stories informing, 27, 52, 68; Taoist, 31, 99; therapists work within societal, 32, 33, 37; therapy on, 35; values relation to, 27, 28–29, 66–67
worry, 34

Yalom, Irvin, 78

About the Authors

Raphael J. Becvar, retired distinguished professor and endowed chair in marital and family therapy, was a licensed psychologist, licensed marriage and family therapist, and an approved supervisor with many years of experience in both academic and private-practice contexts. He has authored and coauthored many books and articles in professional journals. His particular focus is on philosophical and metaperspectives on mental health and the practice of therapy, and he is a widely recognized teacher of systems theory and family therapy.

Dorothy Stroh Becvar, professor emerita in the School of Social Work at St. Louis University, was a licensed marital and family therapist and a licensed clinical social worker. She published extensively, presented workshops, and taught courses, both nationally and internationally, on a wide variety of topics. She was also president and CEO of the Haelan Centers, a not-for-profit corporation dedicated to promoting growth and wholeness in body, mind, and spirit. Dorothy died on August 31, 2021.

Lynne V. Reif, licensed professional counselor, began her career working with at-risk youth in the foster-care system. In 2000, she became a middle school counselor and continued in that role until 2023. Lynne has extensive background in working with children and families and was a part of the leadership team that created and ran the Empowering Young Women conferences hosted by the University of Missouri, St. Louis, for 20 years. In 2012, she traveled to Uganda to coteach a first-of-its-kind course in school counseling to educators there and to work with girls in the schools. This experience deeply expanded her cultural awareness and understanding of the significance of context in the lives of children and families.

www.ingramcontent.com/pod-product-compliance
Lightning Source LLC
Chambersburg PA
CBHW071747270326
41928CB00013B/2825